ADVANCE PRAISE FOR
UPGRADE

"Michael Catt has refused to take the easy road of routines and ruts and call them a walk with God. His prophetic prose reveals a heart softened by the tears streaming from trials and triumph. He has chosen to soar with the Spirit rather than settle for less. Don't be surprised if reading *Upgrade* does the same for you!"

Dr. Gary Miller
TALK LESS! PRAY MORE!

"Michael Catt has taken the very old concept of the victorious Christian life and breathed new life into it. He has 'upgraded' it! Without ignoring the sadness of sin and the rigors of repentance, he has given us hope for the future. The Spirit of God breathes through the pages of this wonderful new book."

Dave Butts
Chairman, America's National Prayer Committee

UPGRADE
FROM ADEQUACY TO ABUNDANCE

MICHAEL CATT

CLC
PUBLICATIONS

Upgrade : from Adequacy to Abundance
© 2012 by Michael Catt
All rights reserved

Published by CLC Publications
PO Box 1449
Fort Washington, PA 19034

ISBN (trade paper): 978-1-936143-21-4
ISBN (e-book): 978-1-936143-92-4

Cover image and design: Sarah Misko

Unless otherwise noted, Scripture quotations are from the New American Standard Bible®, © 1960, 1962, 1963, 1968, 1971, 1972, 1973, 1975, 1977, 1995 by The Lockman Foundation. Used by permission.

Scripture quotations marked NIV are from the Holy Bible, New International Version, ©1973, 1978, 1984 by International Bible Society. Used by permission of Zondervan Bible Publishers.

Italicized words in Scripture quotations are the emphasis of the author.

Printed in the United States of America

20 19 18 17 16 15 14 13 12   1 2 3 4 5 6

DEDICATED TO THE MEMORY OF

James A. Stewart

Author, revivalist, evangelist and founder of Revival Literature. His books have challenged and inspired me through the years to long for the upgraded life of fullness in the Holy Spirit. Although he died in 1975, about the time I was beginning to grasp those truths, his writings still speak to me.

CONTENTS

PREFACE

These chapters were originally birthed in my heart as sermons on what some call "the deeper Christian life," "the victorious Christian life," "the Spirit-filled life" or "the overcoming life." Whatever you call it, unfortunately most believers aren't living it. We are living on the right side of Calvary but the wrong side of Pentecost.

The fear of excessive emotion has kept some from living in the fullness of the Holy Spirit. Others have resigned themselves to an "average" Christian life of defeat and monotony. Both are tragic decisions. God designed us for much more than many are experiencing.

As we've pulled these messages together, we've done so with the knowledge that there is a desperate need for the power of the Holy Spirit in our churches. For that to happen, we cannot settle for a second-class faith.

This image of upgrading the Christian life first came to me while listening to the late African American preacher Manuel Scott. He wove the image of flying first-class throughout his message. I've long since lost that tape, but I remember the truths.

There's nothing new here, but it may be new to you. Or it may be a truth you've known but not appropriated. May the Lord stir your heart in the reading of these chapters as He did mine in preparing them. It is my prayer that these simple truths will have a profound impact on your life.

ACKNOWLEDGMENTS

Without a supportive church, no pastor would ever have the time to write books. Without a competent staff, a pastor would find it impossible to meet every demand of church life. Without time alone in the study, a pastor cannot have a word from the Word for his people.

I am grateful to Laura Pollard from CLC for providing vital editing and flow to these pages. I'm thankful for her diligence and desire to get it right. This is my fourth book with CLC Publications, and I'm blessed by their confidence in my work.

Without Stephanie Bennett and Debbie Toole, I would never get a thing done. Stephanie is my research assistant and always edits my work. Since I can't diagram a sentence, it's important to have someone who can work with me on these books. Debbie manages my schedule, allowing me to have time to write. She's the guard at the door of my office and study. If she had a dollar for every time she's said, "He's not available right now," she would be rich. These ladies are more vital to my ministry than I can ever express on paper.

I'm humbled and grateful for the support of Jim McBride and Bill Reeves who help me with all the details of my publishing. I have long desired to write books and have never been interested in the business side of it all. They've relieved me of that pressure.

I've saved the best for last—my bride, Terri, who has walked with me on this journey since 1974. She has allowed me to head off to my study and stay for hours, waiting patiently for me. She knows my struggles and my longings. She's been there with me through the extraordinary days and the ordinary days.

WHAT'S KEEPING YOU FROM YOUR UPGRADE?

SIN

PICTURE yourself seated in front of a computer. You're frustrated because the system keeps crashing, and you don't know how to fix it. In fact everything you try seems to make the situation worse. Just as you drop your head onto your desk in defeat, the office's information technology specialist (affectionately known as "the IT man") knocks on your door and asks if you'd like him to upgrade your software and solve your problem. You reply with a quick, "No, thank you. I'm fine with what I have," and go back to stressing over your computer troubles.

Many Christians are in a similar situation. They know their fallen human natures are messed up systems and that they need a God override. They are aware of God's love and provision, yet rather than accept them, they allow themselves to be unproductive and continually return to the same sin patterns. Defeat is their standard operating procedure.

I admit that I'm not a tech guy. The IT guy on our staff is a lifesaver for me. Left to myself, I'd probably still be using dial-up. The good news is that someone came along and developed methods and technologies that allow me to work faster and smarter. Such technology is available to all of us, but the sad reality is that some of us are either ignorant of it or refuse to make the effort or pay the price to get the help we need.

It's not that the deeper life is only for an elite few but that many refuse to appropriate what is available. The price has already been paid; God offers these "spiritual upgrades" for free. To not grow in maturity would be to remain as babies in the church nursery. While the Holy Spirit comes into our lives at the point of conversion, there is much more to understand and embrace. Christ calls us to follow Him, and there are stages of development along that road.

So why are you waiting? Your upgrade is available. Why continue living a frustrated, defeated life? The Holy Spirit is living within you and empowering you to live an upgraded life.

When you're dealing with computers, you need to have an operating system that can handle all the benefits of the upgrade. My computer automatically upgrades my virus protection, but if I were running an old virus protection package, I would be in danger of being hacked or having my files corrupted. When we walk in the Spirit, we have the ongoing protection plan provided by the Father. The Holy Spirit guides us into all truth. We are aware of the viruses, scams and other dangers the enemy sends our way to corrupt our lives.

When Jesus died and rose again from the dead, He purchased my upgrade. I have access to the Holy Spirit's power. I no longer live by keeping rules but by abiding in His righteousness. I'm called to die to myself and accept a new, abundant life in Christ.

When you allow Christ to rule in your heart, He will transform you from the inside out. While you may want that upgrade, you can miss out on it by being disqualified. You can't obtain the rewards of a full life in Christ if you don't understand and meet the prerequisites. The Holy Spirit doesn't operate in a vacuum. Just as having an outdated computer system will prevent you from being able to use the newest, best software, refusing to have your life completely transformed by the Lord will prevent you from living in His fullness. There is something that will keep you from "upgrading" to a complete life in Christ—sin.

GETTING CLEAN

When you walk down the household goods aisle of a store, you see dozens of cleaning products. You find items to remove stains from clothes, grease from ovens, and germs from toilets, but no matter how hard you look, you won't find anything that gets rid of sin. Sin is not a surface issue, and it can't be approached casually.

God had to do something very specific and costly to take care of our sin problem: He sent His only Son as a sacrifice in our place. Because of the redemptive work of Jesus Christ's death on the cross, sin has no power in our lives. But as naturally sinful beings, we still struggle with what to do with our sin. No matter where we are in our Christian walk, sin will hold us back from a close relationship with the Lord.

Sinfulness is not a topic we like to think about in our pleasure-seeking society. In today's world, everyone is "spiritual," and nobody talks about sin. In fact many people seek out churches that do not talk about sin. Attempting (often subconsciously) to avoid feelings of guilt and inadequacy, believers and unbelievers alike try to mask or ignore their shortcomings. We've redefined sin to make us feel better about ourselves, but *we are still sinners*.

In order to realize the extent of God's grace and to live a full life in Him, we must first recognize that we have sinned and fallen short of His perfection (Rom. 3:23). Ignoring sinfulness does not negate its reality. Pretending we have it all together is no substitute for the Lord working within us. Only by repenting of our sin against God can we be eligible to advance to His next level for us (Luke 13:3, 5).

Don't write off a discussion of sin as rudimentary. Turning away from sin is easier said than done. Ask the Lord to reveal places in your life in which you're still trapped by sin. How can you, through Christ's power, find full freedom?

RECOGNIZING SIN

The first step in dealing with sin is being aware of it. It requires you to be God-honest. God sees and knows everything, so there's no fooling Him.

Years ago I heard missionary Bertha Smith talk about making a "sin list." She encouraged her audience to write out every sin we could think of. At first I thought my list wouldn't be very long. But before I was through, I had covered a piece of paper front and back.

Ask the Lord to help you view sin as He does. Ask Him to dig deep and open your eyes to see what's holding you back (Ps. 139:23–24). *Lord, make me sensitive to anything that intrudes, influences or impacts my life in a way that isn't pleasing to You. Show me anything in my life that is contrary to Your will.* This is not an easy prayer to pray, but it's the only way to qualify for the life you long to have.

When you're open to letting God speak to you about the sins that slow you down, grind you down and wear you down, you'll find that sin is much more than a surface problem. When you examine your life through the lens of Scripture, you will be humbled by your depravity and by God's grace in constantly loving you.

The Lord desires intimacy, and in order to maintain fellowship with Him, you need to know how to deal with sin. Proverbs 28:13 offers us two choices: "He who conceals his transgressions will not prosper, but he who confesses and forsakes [them] will find compassion." We can conceal sin, or we can confess and conquer it.

CONCEALING SIN

When you were a teenager, did you ever try to hide something—like a bad report card or a broken vase—from your parents? We often try to do the same with God—covering our faults and insecurities by pretending we have it all together—but this never works.

Some people will never receive an upgrade because of "secret" sins. With the blessings of technology also come the evils of technology. Far too many believers are caught in the web of pornography. Others have inappropriate conversations with the opposite sex on social networks. Failing to maintain a filter will lead to viruses and malware that can and will destroy your soul.

When I was a teenager, I wasn't saved, and I tried to fit in with the wrong crowd. Though I went to church every week, I wasn't living for Christ. I remember one occasion when I purchased some alcohol and hid it in the trunk of my car. I thought I had covered it up. I was awakened on Saturday morning by my dad grabbing my T-shirt and pulling me toward his face, asking, "Where did that beer come from?" What I thought was hidden had been found by my father when he searched my car.

Hiding sin isn't a new phenomenon. Time and time again we see biblical characters trying to keep their disobedience from being exposed. Let's look at a few examples.

Adam and Eve tried to downplay their sin by placing blame. Adam said the sin was Eve's fault (and God's fault for having created her): "The woman whom You gave to be with me, she gave me from the tree" (Gen. 3:12). Eve claimed she wasn't acting on her own volition: "The serpent deceived me" (Gen. 3:13).

Cain killed his brother, and when God asked him where Abel was, he responded, "'I do not know. Am I my brother's keeper?'" (Gen. 4:9)

Ananias and Sapphira lied about the price of the land they sold, attempting to appear more holy by claiming they had given all their profits to the church. They were both struck down because of their desire to hide the truth.

These may seem like extreme examples, but we too try to conceal our sins. Have you ever, for example, lied to your spouse about where you've been? Let someone else take the blame for what you did wrong? Taken supplies from your office? Stolen time at work by not doing the job you are paid to do? Just fill in the blank: I was involved in a cover-up when I _____. There are many little ways in which we make our lives miserable and make others' lives more difficult. We think we can cheat the system, but in the end we cheat ourselves of joy unspeakable.

It isn't enough to go to church once a week or even to have daily devotions; we have to humble ourselves before God and not attempt to justify our sins. You can be a dedicated churchgoer and still a grade-A sinner. First John 1:6 says, "If we say that we have fellowship with Him and [yet] walk in the darkness, we lie and do not practice the truth."

Concealing sin is not hypocritical; it's duplicitous. In other words, when we try to hide our sin, we lie not only to others but also to ourselves: "If we say that we have no sin, we are deceiving ourselves and the truth is not in us" (1:8).

The Bible identifies us as fallen, sinful beings, so if we claim we're sinless, we reject the truth of God's Word: "If we say that we have not sinned, we make Him a liar and His word is not in us" (1:10). Denying sin is a sin in itself. When you falsely claim to be pure and holy, you lie to yourself and worse—you assert that God is a liar.

Note the downward spiral in the verses from First John: verse 6 says we aren't living by the truth; verse 8 says the truth is not in us; and verse 10 says the Word has no place in our lives. God takes sin seriously. Hiding sin distances us from God and keeps Him from operating within us. The pattern of concealing sin leads from rejecting the truth to being separated from God's Word. Pretending you're perfect has serious repercussions.

Take David for example. Knowing he was committing sin, David seduced Bathsheba, the wife of Uriah the Hittite, and then had Uriah killed by sending him to the front lines of battle. David kept outwardly silent about his acts and intentions for a year, but inwardly he was torn apart. Trying to cover up his sins negatively impacted every major area of his life.

Psalm 51 offers a glimpse into the multiple afflictions David suffered as a result of covering up his disobedience.

His mind was affected. Sin is not solely a spiritual issue; it also takes a mental toll. David recognized that refusing to admit his sin was like lying to God, and he noted that this went against the Lord's desire for "truth in the innermost being" (51:6). That's why Paul called us to have a renewed mind (Rom. 12:1–2).

His body was affected. In verse 8 David pleaded, "Let the bones which you have broken rejoice." His sin made it feel as if his very bones had been busted. The psalmist's vision and hearing also suffered. He grieved that his sin was ever before him in verse 3. In verse 8 he asked to be made to "hear joy and gladness"—to be freed from listening to his own lamentations. There is no joy in the life of sin.

His heart was affected. Recognizing his own depravity, David was pained and made aware of his need for renewal. His prayer in verse 10 was, "Create in me a clean heart, O God, and renew a steadfast spirit within me."

His peace was affected. David's afflictions left him in a constant state of unrest. Finally admitting his wrongdoing to the Lord, he begged for mercy: "Do not cast me away from Your presence and do not take Your Holy Spirit from me" (51:11). Millions of people are in counseling today because they have no peace. More than needing pills or a psychiatrist, they need a purifying that will address the root of the unrest in their lives.

His joy was affected. After petitioning God to maintain His presence in his life, David asked to have fullness of joy. David recognized that a mark of a healthy walk with the Lord is being filled with the Lord's gladness. In verse 12 he wrote, "Restore to me the joy of your salvation." I see a lot of believers who lack joy. They look miserable, and their faces reflect bitterness, anger, fear, anxiety—but little joy.

His will was affected. Because of the callousness that comes from concealing sin (which involves the repeated rejection of God's renewing grace), David found himself growing defiant. Looking forward, he asked God, "Sustain me with a willing spirit" (51:12).

David's "hidden" sin tore his life apart. And the sin wasn't really hidden. It was like a virus that, though you may not see it when you open the e-mail, won't take long to disrupt and infect your system.

When David was finally confronted by the prophet Nathan, he recognized that only God could save him from his situation, he cried out to God to restore him: "Deliver me from bloodguiltiness, O God, the God of my salvation; then my tongue will joyfully sing of Your righteousness. O Lord, open my lips, that my mouth may declare Your praise" (51:14–15).

Sin cannot be ignored and forgotten. Instead it must be recognized and renounced. God will only work when we give our-

selves over to be used by Him. The first step to a right relationship with God is admitting that we have sinned.

CONFESSING SIN

Few books have impacted my life more than *The Calvary
Road* by Roy Hession. It was incredibly convicting to me when
I first read it in the 1970s. I can still recall the night I confessed
to my wife that I wasn't the man I was supposed to be. It was
painful, but it was also liberating.

Even the slightest sin, like the smallest cancer, can destroy
you if you refuse to confess it. When you stop concealing your
sin, you free yourself from the "accuser of the brethren." But
this is not the same as *confessing*—or admitting to yourself and
God that you have sinned. To "confess" means "to say the same
thing." In other words, when you confess, you say the same thing
about your sin that God does. You call your sin sin.

No matter what label you put on it—big sin, little sin, sin
of omission, sin of commission—you need to clean it out of
your life in order to restore a right relationship with Christ.
God isn't interested in excuses and explanations; He only
wants you to agree with the evidence—to admit that you have
sinned!

First John 1:9 may be one of the best known and least ap-
plied verses in the Bible: "If we confess our sins, He is faithful
and righteous to forgive us our sins and to cleanse us from all
unrighteousness." This verse contains a conditional clause. We
have already been forgiven because Christ blotted out our sins,
but we need *constant* cleansing. You don't confess your sins to
maintain your salvation; you confess to keep it up-to-date. You
confess to enjoy the blessings and benefits of being saved!

I am a strong proponent of the altar call. Why? Because if
we aren't willing to bow before God and admit our desperate

need of Him, we can easily hide behind our religious facades. A computer can be perfectly clean on the outside and have a crisp, high-definition display—yet it may be full of viruses. We too can look holy while being corrupt on the inside. We need to humble ourselves before the Lord. Sometimes an inner cleaning demands a public declaration of spiritual bankruptcy. David did it, and we admire him for it. Why then do we resist it so much?

Confessing is not necessarily begging God to forgive you; it's simply agreeing with God that you're a sinner. When you confess your sin, you need to strive not to water down or compare your sin with another's (e.g. "I just lied. It's not like I murdered anyone.") Admit your sin—call it like it is—and don't try to lessen it through comparison.

The book *Whatever Happened to Sin* claims that we have cleaned up the language we use to talk about sin to make it sound more acceptable. We now use words that sound more politically correct and that are in line with pop psychology. But until we're willing to say the same thing about sin that God does, there will be no deliverance.

So what does confession look like?

Confession is continual. Look at First John 1:9 again. This verse is all about taking God at His word and having faith that He will restore you. The moment you're aware of your sin, confess the way(s) in which you've turned your back on God's truths, and He will immediately forgive you. If you want daily victory, there should be daily confession. Keep your "sin list" short.

Confession is complete. Specific sins require specific confessions. You can't just mutter a quick, "Forgive me for all my sins, amen" and be done with it. That's not a confession; that's a cop-out. Ask God to reveal the precise ways in which you've broken fellowship with Him and then seek His pardon for each one. You must honestly face your sins, or you'll never be able to honestly face your Savior. If it requires asking someone else to forgive you, do it.

Confession is confident. I see a lot of Christians today struggling with guilt. Even though God has forgiven them, they can't seem to forgive themselves. They drag around garbage and baggage from their past instead of living in Christ's freedom. The Holy Spirit will never convict you of a sin He has already forgiven; the devil is the one who dredges up the past and lays guilt trips on you. Many people confess their sins but then live in doubt, wondering if God ever really forgave them. The Bible teaches, however, that God "pardons all your iniquities" (Ps. 103:3). We need to take God at His Word. If you keep asking God to forgive you for things you did in the past, you basically call Him a liar by assuming He's not "faithful and righteous to forgive" (1 John 1:9).

Thankfully, God gives us unmerited, abundant grace—not what we deserve. Psalm 103:10–12 reads, "He has not dealt with us according to our sins, nor rewarded us according to our iniquities. For as high as the heavens are above the earth, so great is His loving-kindness toward those who fear Him. As far as the east is from the west, so far has He removed our transgressions from us." Note that the Lord separates your sin from you as far as the east is from the west. God keeps no record of wrongs and won't rehash your past sins. When He forgives, you are completely freed.

God is faithful to His Word and acts justly toward us because of His Son. When you confess your sins, Christ acts as your advocate—as your heavenly lawyer—asserting that you are innocent because of His sacrifice. "My little children, I am writing these things to you so that you may not sin. And if anyone sins, we have an Advocate with the Father, Jesus Christ the righteous; and He Himself is the propitiation for our sins; and not for ours only, but also for those of the whole world" (1 John 2:1).

A great spiritual giant in my life, the late Ron Dunn, told me, "In heaven, in the very presence of the heavenly Father, even though I am so sinful and wretched and wicked, there is One pleading my case." Ron taught me that Christ is my advocate, my lawyer. I can trust my lawyer because: (1) The judge is His father, so they never rule against one another. (2) He's in good standing with the court. Christ is completely righteous and has already paid the price for our crimes against Holy God. Think about it—Christ doesn't plead our innocence; He pleads His own blood. Irrefutable evidence that guilt has been removed!

Praise the Lord that when you confess your sins, He has both the ability and the desire to pardon them.

> Who is a God like you, who pardons iniquity and passes over the rebellious act of the remnant of His possession? He does not retain His anger forever, because He delights in unchanging love. He will again have compassion on us; He will tread our iniquities under foot. Yes, You will cast all their sins into the depths of the sea. (Micah 7:18–20)

Because of God's promise to cleanse you from sin, you can be confident in your confession.

CONQUERING SIN

Sin destroys lives and eats away at relationships, but the good news is that, as believers in Christ Jesus, we can have victory over sin. Christ offers total, continual triumph. We don't have to live like yo-yo Christians—confessing our sins at the altar and then going right back to the same lifestyle—because we have been set free!

The major disqualifying factor for our upgrade has already been nullified, but many fail to embrace this truth. We highlight words and passages in our Bibles like "more than conquerors," "overcomers," "victory" and "power," but we live as if the power is out and we've been overrun by a stronger enemy. Everything the devil accuses you of might be true, but when you plead the blood of the Lamb over your situation, your scarlet sins are made white as snow.

You cannot do anything to defeat sin in your own power, but Jesus can wash you clean. Romans 8:1 reminds us that "there is now no condemnation for those who are in Christ Jesus," and First John 1:7 echoes, "the blood of Jesus His Son cleanses us from all sin." Sin has been conquered through Christ! Because of this, we are able to walk in the light. There are two different ways in which being in the light is accomplished.

First, we're guided by the light of God's Word. The psalmist proclaimed, "Thy Word is a lamp unto my feet and a light unto my path" (119:105). Vance Havner, a great prophet of the twentieth century, once said in a sermon,

> If I've heard it once, I've heard it countless times, "It all depends on how you look at it." Nothing depends on how we look at it. That would be the last verse of the book of Judges all over again with every man doing that which is right in his own eyes. That is anarchy, with every man his own judge, and we are in the midst of that sad state today. Everything depends on how God looks at it, and what He says about it in His Word.

Second, we are able to walk in God's light through worship of Him, "for to worship God is to quicken the conscience with the holiness of God, feed the mind with the truth of God, purge the conscience with the beauty of God, open the heart to the love of God, devote the will to the service of God."[1] This worship involves Christian fellowship. You can't conquer sin in isolation; you need to be in the body with your brothers and sisters in Christ. First John 1:7 reminds us, "If we walk in the Light as He Himself is in the Light, we have fellowship with one another, and the blood of Jesus His Son cleanses us from all sin."

HOLD ONTO THAT UPGRADE!

I used to have stacks of floppy discs for my programs, but I finally had to throw them away because new computers store data differently. It would be silly to continue using outmoded technology since better options are available. Upgrades necessitate abandoning the old way of doing things.

You can't enjoy the functions of the newer version until you trade in your outdated model. Once you've been set free by Christ, you no longer have to answer to your sin nature. Sin doesn't have the power to control what the Lord has made new, so live like the repurposed creature you are!

Refusing to Repent

I HAVE a type A personality. I'm also a prophet (forth-telling as in spreading the truth, not foretelling as in predicting things to come). In other words, I don't deal with gray zones. I see everything in black and white.

Even though I search for what's right, I have a hard time admitting when I'm wrong. It can be incredibly difficult for me to apologize. I'd risk saying that one of the hardest things for people to genuinely say is "I'm sorry. I messed up. It's my fault." People sue cigarette companies for their lung cancer and complain that fast-food places make them gain weight. We are a nation of victims who like to lay blame rather than take personal responsibility. "It's not my fault!" is the resonating cry.

You find this blame ideology everywhere. *Time* magazine published an article on August 15, 1994, titled, "Infidelity: It may be in our genes." The piece justified adultery on the grounds that we are genetically preprogrammed to be unfaithful. Although we'd all agree that negative environments can cause people to act certain ways, the reality is that we need to understand the responsibilities that come along with our life choices.

Yet blame is the name of the game these days. In this blame culture, the thought of accepting responsibility for mistakes is unheard of. I really enjoyed a Doonsebury cartoon that addressed this problem. The first panel showed a professor standing in front of his class, explaining that anyone who wanted to claim victim status on the basis of "race, gender, ethnicity, sexual preference or disability" to avoid being graded on merit on the next project should do so by the end of the week. He says, "If you do not register your status as a victim by that time, you will not be able to claim preferential treatment." A voice in the back of the room asks, "What about the time impaired? Doesn't setting a deadline discriminate against them?" The professor then responds, "Of course. Exceptions will be made for the totally clueless."

We find this cartoon humorous because we've experienced what it's parodying. It's become so uncommon to admit shortcomings that we list off excuses when something goes wrong, refusing to acknowledge that we might be the ones at fault.

It's easy to admit the big problems in our culture, but let's move a little closer to home. Think about how the American church functions. Flipping through church channels on TV, I'm often struck by how *bored* the people in congregations look. They sit there yawning and dozing off, their arms folded in disinterest. They show no evidence of the joy and victory of the Spirit-filled life. Most don't even have their Bibles out. Then add to that what you don't see on television: empty altars, people leaving during the invitation, flippant conversations in the foyer immediately after a word from the Word. No wonder our churches are in such terrible condition.

Nothing is more unattractive than lifeless, tradition-stuck religion. The children of such churchgoers see more life in bars

than in the church. According to numerous studies over the last
three decades, the overwhelming majority of kids raised in the
church leave and don't come back. The research shows that a
powerless church produces an apathetic generation.

The world isn't interested in piety; it's interested in a Savior with skin on. When you're saturated with the Holy Spirit—
when the Lord's goodness is almost oozing out of you—people
will be attracted to Christ in you.

Of course, this transformation isn't as easy as flipping a
switch from joyless to joyful. Because the problem is not that
the dull churchgoers I mentioned above refuse to worship; it's
that they *can't*. You can't sing when your lips are locked with sin.
You can't dance on the broken feet of rebellion.

You'll never be a worshiper until you're a confessor. Humbling yourself before God comes before a shouted hallelujah!
You have to accept your brokenness in order to move into a place
of blessing.

You won't find many books on brokenness because no one
really likes to talk about it. Sure, there are a few. Nancy Leigh
DeMoss wrote an excellent book called *Brokenness: The Heart
God Revives*. I dealt with the issue in my book *The Power of Des-
peration*. But you won't find a section on brokenness or repentance in your local bookstore. The subject just doesn't sell.

Christians use the word repentance to talk about the act of
humbly turning away from sin. Evangelical repentance starts
when you recognize your own sinfulness and realize the magni-
tude and mercy of Christ's sacrifice. According to *Easton's Bible
Dictionary*, "The true penitent is conscious of guilt (Ps. 51:4, 9),
of pollution (51:5, 7, 10), and of helplessness (51:11; 109:21,
22). Thus he apprehends himself to be just what God has always seen him to be and declares him to be."[2] Within this model
there's no room for excuses or blame. You have to get your heart

right before God before you can follow His commandments. You won't have joy until you surrender to His Spirit—and that involves admitting that you have sinned and that you don't have it all together.

Refusing to repent ruins your chances for an upgrade. It's like deciding you're going to walk the entire way across the country when you're only a couple frequent-flier miles away from the platinum business elite class just because you don't like the idea of having to take your shoes off at security. Because you don't want to submit yourself to scrutiny, you choose a subpar form of transportation. I'm not trying to say you should fly more. What I am saying is that there's no reason to settle for less than the best God has for you.

God has placed a calling on your life, and He longs for you to draw closer to Him through repentance. Don't miss out on the joy and blessing waiting on the other side of your stubbornness and rebellion.

Admit You're Unclean

Look at David. David knew what it meant to have a heart for God. But he lost the joy of the Lord because he committed adultery and had a hand in murder—yet pretended nothing was wrong. David was not only self-indulgent, he was self-deluded. He thought he could control his situation, but he couldn't. He thought he wasn't accountable for his actions, but he was. He thought he wouldn't get caught, but he did.

As David learned, sin always takes you further than you intend to go, and it leads to more serious complications and deceptions. When you live for yourself—not following the path God has laid out for you—you invite more and more sin into your life. And the farther down the path of rebellion you go, the more difficult it is to turn around.

Recognizing and admitting you're living the wrong way is incredibly difficult. It touches upon issues of privacy, pride and self-dependence. It demands honesty and vulnerability.

When people are struggling with hidden sin, they typically respond to fellow Christians in one of three ways. They either (1) become apathetic, inactive and indifferent to the things of God—slipping further and further away from fellowship (2) continue going to church and try to rationalize their behavior, which hardens their hearts to the Word or (3) attack anything or anyone that convicts them of their sin. Don't let yourself fall into any of these patterns! Instead, focus on living in a right and clean relationship with the Lord. Listen to those who love you enough to confront you with a loving rebuke.

Are you currently ruining your chances for a faith upgrade by holding onto sin? The key to relational success with the Lord is being transparent and willing to be transformed into His like-ness—and sin keeps you from looking anything like your Savior.

Don't Deny Your Nathan!

You should thank God when He sends someone into your life to get you out of the ditch of your own sinfulness. Saul made excuses when he was confronted by a prophet. David didn't. That's the difference between the possibility of an upgraded and renewed experience with Christ and seeing the hand of God re-moved from your life.

Although it can be hard to swallow, godly rebuke is often necessary. When you study the ministry of the prophets and of Jesus, you see that avoiding hurt feelings is far from a priority. Whether you like it or not, you need a prophetic voice in your life—someone who will tell you the truth even when it hurts.[3]

For David, this person was Nathan. Nathan came into David's life with the bare knuckles of honesty and confronted

David about the sin he'd been trying to hide. Because of his disobedience, David had been unable to praise, and his harp had been out of tune for over a year. At the end of this psalmless period, God sent Nathan to confront David to get his life back on track.

In Second Samuel 12 Nathan went to David and told him a story of two men—one rich and one poor. Nathan explained that the poor man had nothing except one sheep that was like a member of the family. When the rich man had a traveler come to visit him, he was unwilling to kill one of his own flock, so he took the poor man's sheep and had it prepared for dinner.

Upon hearing of this injustice, David became angry and declared that the rich man deserved to pay the poor man back four times what he owed him and even deserved to die! David set himself up for his fall, and Nathan was ready to deliver.

Nathan then said to David,

> You are the man! Thus says the LORD God of Israel, "It is I who anointed you king over Israel and it is I who delivered you from the hand of Saul. I also gave you your master's house and your master's wives into your care, and I gave you the house of Israel and Judah; and if that had been too little, I would have added to you many more things like these! Why have you despised the word of the LORD by doing evil in His sight? You have struck down Uriah the Hittite with the sword, have taken his wife to be your wife, and have killed him with the sword of the sons of Ammon." (12:7–9)

Although David performed his sins in secret, the Lord was aware of them. When Nathan laid them bare, David confessed what he should have admitted from the very beginning: "I have sinned against the LORD" (12:13). David recognized that while his sins took place in the physical world, they were ultimately against God.

I have to give David credit. He was honest, and that's more than I can say for a lot of Christians. He may have been a great sinner, but David was an even greater repenter. When confronted with his sin, he didn't place blame or deny his actions. Rather than demanding his rights or hiding behind his title, he bared his heart to the Lord and declared, "I will confess my transgressions to the LORD" (Ps. 32:5). He accepted the weight of what he had done, and while he recognized he couldn't undo his past, he knew God could and would forgive him.

Unfortunately, most of my peers who were in ministry when I started are no longer in ministry, and they are living far below where they should be. I can name at least three who I confronted about serious issues. My confrontation was met with either indifference or defensiveness. After years of trying to help, I had to shake the dust off and move on. It still saddens me to think of what those men could have been.

God is the best forgiver in the history of the universe, but to receive His pardon, we have to accept His rebuke—no matter whom He chooses to deliver it!

THE BEAUTY OF A BROKEN SPIRIT

Broken spirits allow God to receive the glory He deserves. According to Psalm 32:17, God treasures a man with a penitent heart. "The sacrifices of God are a broken spirit, a broken and contrite heart, O God, You will not despise." Through brokenness, you learn the value and necessity of obedience. The Lord does not desire lip service and false promises; instead He asks for repentance and humility.

God knows the real state of your heart; everything is laid bare to Him. Hebrews 4:12–13 tells us,

> The Word of God is living and active and sharper than any two-edged sword, and piercing as far as the division of soul and spirit,

of both joints and marrow, and able to judge the thoughts and intentions of the heart. And there is no creature hidden from His sight, but all things are open and laid bare to the eyes of Him.

God knows exactly where you stand. Do you?

Because the Lord already knows your struggles and your failings, there's no use in trying to hide them to maintain some false pretense of control. God delights in those who are honest, real and aware of their fallen state.

The signs of a broken spirit are all beautifully displayed in the psalmist's return to His Lord. First, *David recognized the majesty of God.* After the confrontation with Nathan, David wrote Psalm 51 as a plea for pardon. He compared God's abundance to his poverty and the depths of God's love to his shallowness and self-centeredness. Accepting his own fallen state allowed David to more fully worship God for His goodness and greatness.

David recognized the justice of God. In Psalm 51:4 David admitted, "Against You, You only, I have sinned and done what is evil in Your sight, so that You are justified when You speak and blameless when You judge." David recognized that he was unworthy to be pardoned, and he thanked the Lord for whatever decision He made. Rather than operating on situational ethics and attempting to justify his situation, David turned to the ultimate source of honest and holy justice.

David recognized the mercy of God. Although God's justice does not demand mercy, David knew that his God was a God of mercy. David pleaded, "Have mercy on me, O God" (Ps. 51:1, NIV). Grace is something that God has freely bestowed on us, and we don't deserve it, so we can't claim it. Like David we can, however, fall before the Lord and ask for mercy.

God had left David to his life of compromise and sin, and David wasted away both spiritually and physically. Sometimes the punishment for sin is sin. God gives us the freedom to choose our path, but we can't always choose where it will lead us. In order to get back to the promise of what the Lord had for him, David had to admit he had been unfaithful and unrighteous and that he was unable to restore himself. In verse 16 he revealed his awareness of being unable to atone for his own sins: "You delight not in sacrifice, or I would bring it; You do not take pleasure in burnt offerings."

To get back to the Lord's favor—to qualify for a spiritual upgrade, so to speak—you must humble yourself and allow your spirit to be broken.

BENEFITS OF A BROKEN SPIRIT

It may sound strange to think of profiting from being broken, but when selfish pride and physical desires are removed from the equation, God is able to work. Failure doesn't have to be fatal or final. He is the God of second chances. And when the Lord is in control, He'll give you what is *best* for your life.

So what does it look like when you're honest with God and allow Him to deal with you in the innermost parts of your being? What happens when you allow the Holy Spirit to do His healing work in your heart and to renew you?

For starters, *you'll have a clean heart.* Just as high blood pressure, high cholesterol and smoking can lead to physical heart problems, the way you handle sin impacts your spiritual heart. In Psalm 51:10 David asked of the Lord, "Create in me a clean heart, O God, and renew a steadfast spirit within me."

When I was a pastor in Ada, Oklahoma, I received a phone call that made my breath catch. The voice on the other end of the line told me that my father had suffered a serious heart attack. That night was a blur. We threw a few changes of clothes in the car and drove to Mississippi. We were only able to visit a few moments in the cardiac care unit, but they were precious.

Before we reached home, we got a call telling us Dad was being transferred to a hospital with a cardiac specialist. He had four blocked arteries and needed surgery. In other words, his heart was clogged up.

The truth is that we all have sin clogging our hearts, and spiritual open heart surgery is far from as common as it should be. But the good news is that we don't have to live with that blockage, waiting for it to destroy us. Psalm 51 explains that God creates clean hearts in us!

Another benefit of having a broken spirit is that *you'll experience new assurance in your faith*. Verse 11 promises that God won't be a distant deity; He'll be the closest, best Father anyone could ever have.

You will have a steadfast spirit. Having Christ in your life also allows you to experience stability. David asks the Lord to "renew a steadfast spirit within me" (51:10). Once your spirit has been humbled, you can rest in Christ; He *never* fails.

When you stand firm on God's promises and are certain of your faith, *you will display true joy.* In 51:12 David petitioned God, "Restore to me the joy of Your salvation." David knew that joy is a by-product of a right walk with the Lord. When Christ has first place in your life, your entire countenance will glow with His presence. The type of joy He offers isn't one that depends on laughable moments or happy occasions; it's a joy that is rooted deep within, untouched by exterior circumstances.

You'll be able to center on this joy as *you develop an entirely new attitude.* In verse 17 David explained, "The sacrifices of God are a broken spirit..." It's important to be humble—not to have a cocky, arrogant, independent spirit.

In addition to this new attitude about life, *you will enjoy a new attitude concerning worship.* When the clot is removed from your heart, you will be lifted out of the mire of sin and into a choir of praise. After having his life perspective readjusted, David announced that he would sing to the Lord: "My tongue will joyfully sing of Your righteousness. O Lord, open my lips, that my mouth may declare Your praise" (51:14–15).

When you follow God with a submissive spirit, you are then able to speak truth into others' lives. *You will receive a new ministry.* God used David to bring others to Himself. In verse 13 David proclaimed, "Then I will teach transgressors Your ways, and sinners will be converted to You." Even today, thousands of years later, David still speaks to us. We can learn from the records of his honesty, confession, repentance and renewed walk with Jehovah.

When you live in a self-humbling, ministry-fulfilling way, allowing God to control each step, *you will gain a right perspective.* Your eye doctor may have told you that you have 20/20 vision, but you aren't seeing correctly if you don't want to give back for all the great things you have received. When you're right with God, you see giving an offering as a part of worship, and you understand the necessity of monetary sacrifice. David emphasized this concept of giving back to the Lord in Psalm 51:17–19: "By Your favor do good to Zion; build the walls of Jerusalem. Then You will delight in righteous sacrifice, in burnt offering and whole burnt offering; then young bulls will be offered on Your altar." One reason people never experience an upgraded life is because they rob God of the glory He's due. Because all things come from Him, God deserves *all* praise and expressions of our thankfulness!

Having a broken spirit isn't about being dejected and walking around complaining about how miserable you are; it's about getting yourself out of God's way so that He can use you in the ways He has planned. When you confess your sin and accept His forgiveness, you will be struck by His grace, and a song of joy and praise will rise up within you.

David offered a praise report after his spirit was renewed:

> When I kept silent about my sin, my body wasted away through my groaning all day long. For day and night Thy hand was heavy upon me; my vitality was drained away as with the fever heat of summer. Selah. I acknowledged my sin to Thee, and my iniquity I did not hide; I said, "I will confess my transgressions to the LORD"; and Thou didst forgive the guilt of my sin. Selah. (Ps. 32:3–5)

Some of the most joyful people I've ever known are those who have been broken by life and then lifted up by the grace of God.

THE NEED FOR REPENTANCE

I do not pastor a church of perfect people. Some folks come to us with a lot of baggage. Some are struggling to give things to Christ that are weighing them down.

But I can look around my church and see people who have been delivered from all kinds of sin—sexual addictions, alcohol addictions, drug addictions, pornography and more—singing songs of praise, taking notes on sermons, and serving in ministry.

The good news of the gospel is that God heals. God *transforms* lives. But to access His healing and fullness, we have to repent.

You don't hear a lot about repentance these days, but that doesn't mean it isn't important. In fact, no one can experience the upgraded life without it. You can't become a Christian and you can't maintain fellowship unless you continually repent.

The word the Bible uses for repentance is the Greek verb *metanoeo*, which comes from *meta*, meaning "after," and *noeo*, "meaning to perceive." The word literally means "to perceive afterwards." Rather than simply meaning hindsight, the word deals with a change of mind, direction and purpose. Through repentance we learn who we are in relation to Christ's truth; we're challenged to evaluate our heart's direction.

In salvation and in sanctification, we are called to first repent and then believe. But the Christian life is more than just belief; it demands action. Repentance is an interior action, but it has exterior results. The prophets preached repentance. John the Baptist preached repentance. Jesus preached repentance. In fact, the last word of Jesus to the church was not the Great Commission (Mark 16:15). To five out of seven churches in Revelation, the command is to "repent; or else . . ." (such as in 2:16).

So what does godly repentance look like? David again offers a good example. His reaction to having his sin exposed was, "Be gracious to me, O God, according to Thy lovingkindness; according to the greatness of Thy compassion blot out my transgressions. Wash me thoroughly from my iniquity, and cleanse me from my sin . . . Make me to hear joy and gladness, let the bones which Thou hast broken rejoice" (Ps. 51:1–2, 8). When David's life became flat and tasteless, he longed for a fresh encounter with the Lord. In Psalm 51 David wasn't asking for an emotional experience or to *feel something*; he sought real intimacy with the almighty God!

Repentance isn't about relief from suffering; it's about seeking righteousness. Revival has its roots in repentance, so we need to take it seriously. It's impossible to enjoy the benefits of an upgraded life in God's kingdom without first repenting.

Repentance begins with a longing to be purified. One reason some of God's people don't find purification is that they only seek relief in a sixty-second trip to the altar. God has a more serious cleaning in mind. In Psalm 51:7 David said to the Lord, "Purify me with hyssop, and I shall be clean; wash me, and I shall be whiter than snow." Hyssop was an herb the Hebrews used in their ceremonial cleansing of lepers. By asking to be purified with hyssop, David was petitioning to be "un-sinned." He wasn't looking for a light scrub or a quick touch-up; he wanted to be clean to the very core of his being.

Cleansing is costly, and it can be difficult to endure. But just like submerging fabrics in boiling water and scrubbing them hard cleans them best, purity demands that the old sinful ways be beaten and wrung out of you.

David chose the picture of broken bones to describe the pain of spiritual separation. Spiritual healing begins when God "sets" your broken heart and broken spirit. It might be painful, but the Lord's cleansing will leave you whiter than snow.

Once you have been purified, you will experience true joy. Note that purification comes before joy; this order can't be reversed. It may seem odd to think of discovering joy through pain, but author Elizabeth Skoglund explains, "In an era of 'Praise the Lord' theology, the real meaning of words like praise and joy may become lost to superficiality. For it is only in deep suffering that people know the depths of all emotion, whether it be pain that is almost unbearable even for one moment or joy that sweeps over the soul once that pain is gone."[4]

David was frustrated, tired of the paralysis of sin, and in need of a radical change in his life. Because he wasn't willing to settle for surface change, David discovered the transforming power of repentance. David asked God to purify him so he could sing joyfully of the Lord's righteousness (51:14). He pled, "Restore to me the joy of Thy salvation" (51:12).

The problem for Christians today isn't that the church is totally dead or that the world has infiltrated the church; it's that we've become comfortable in our compromise. Rather than hating our sin and wholeheartedly longing to be purified, we've taken painkillers to deaden the ache of broken bones. But we don't have to settle for mediocrity.

Revivals can't be planned like the next church meeting. Instead they arise when the individual members of a church humble themselves and pray. Vance Havner wrote, "The church must first repent. God begins His work with His own people. The average church needs to restore the mourner's bench. The first mourners should be the members. When God's people humble themselves and pray and seek God's face, God will send showers of blessing and a harvest of souls."

I remember an old song by the group Truth called "Whatever It Takes" that says,

> Whatever it takes to be more like You,
> That's what I'll be willing to do.
> For whatever it takes, for my will to break,
> That's what I'll be willing to do.

Is this your prayer? Christ will honor your desire to be more like Him, but ascending to that higher level of Christian living involves (1) listening to those godly people who speak truth into your situation and (2) admitting your need for more of God and less of yourself.

Are you desperate to dance before the Lord and praise His name? You can't rejoice and walk in sin, so repent and then thank God for the good work He's going to do in your life.

MEDIOCRITY

IF YOU'VE ever had a Windows computer, you're probably familiar with the warning, "Your antivirus software is about to expire. Would you like to upgrade to the new version?" Viruses are constantly modifying and discovering new ways around the firewalls designed to protect your system. If you delay downloading the updated version, you risk getting a virus capable of destroying everything. If you don't do anything, you opt out of an upgrade and open yourself to attack. The problem here is inaction and delay.

This is also true of the Christian walk. If you aren't pursuing God, chances are you're allowing yourself to stagnate. And when that happens, you don't just stay in the same place; you become infected with "viruses" like greed, lust, envy and laziness. In order to get right with God, you need a total system reboot, and you need to keep your software up-to-date. The Holy Spirit wants to help you take the next step; are you ready to stand up and walk with Him?

THE COLD TRUTH? WE'RE NOT SO HOT

A lie that seems to be propagated by American Christianity is that God accepts—or even is pleased—with halfhearted commitment. While He loves us unconditionally, God calls us in His Word to die to self, take up the cross and confess Jesus as Lord of our lives.

People who are truly on fire for the Lord are frequently labeled as religious nuts. We accept fanatic fans in sports, yet we're often uncomfortable around believers who are totally sold out for Jesus. While we complain when we see players on our favorite football team only giving partial effort, we unashamedly give far less than 100 percent to God. We see average as acceptable. As Vance Havner explained, "Most church members live so far below the standard, you'd have to backslide to be in fellowship."

Jesus dealt with this issue of substandard living in the book of Revelation:

> I know your deeds, that you are neither cold nor hot; I wish that you were cold or hot. So because you are lukewarm, and neither hot nor cold, I will spit you out of My mouth. Because you say, "I am rich, and have become wealthy, and have need of nothing," and you do not know that you are wretched and miserable and poor and blind and naked. (3:15–17)

We're supposed to be *on fire* for God, but we've allowed ourselves to cool to match the temperature around us. E.M. Bounds writes, "Lack of spiritual heat creates more infidelity than lack of faith. Not to be consumingly interested about the things of heaven, is not to be interested at all."[5]

If the ultimate state is to burn for the Lord, what causes the fire to die down? Or maybe—what keeps the flame from ever catching hold of our lives? God's judgment against our churches will be that we have had a lack of zeal, passion and purpose. As long as we consider going to church, entering into true worship, pouring our hearts out to God in prayer, studying the Scriptures, supporting missions, caring for others and having a concern for the lost as *optional*, we'll never make the progress God intended.

Indifference and apathy are just as serious as more active and obvious sins. There's no way to dress up the words of Jesus to Laodicea—the apathetic condition of the church nauseated the Lord. Its members were a little too good to be defined as bad, but they were also too bad to be good. They tried to balance their religion with their reputation and worldly desires, and it sickened Christ. In other words, they wore a façade and played a religious game.

In the verses quoted above from Revelation 3, there are two phrases that reveal the key problems of the Laodicean church. When Jesus explained, "Because you say, 'I am rich . . . and have need of nothing,'" He reflected the high opinion they had of themselves. They took pride in their belongings and status and therefore acted as if they did not need the Lord.

Christ coupled this summary with "And you do not know"—revealing that the church at Laodicea was clueless concerning God's evaluation of them. Because they'd been comparing themselves to other believers and churches and found that they were doing well by the world's standards of success, they failed to realize they were measuring themselves on a faulty scale.

In having everything they wanted, the church at Laodicea missed what they needed—a burning passion for God. Could it be that when we leave church thinking we've had a "good worship service," in reality, we've worshiped a god we've created in *our image* instead of worshiping God as He is?

The church needs an enthusiasm that isn't dependent on emotions or the economy or personal health. Feelings aren't going to get you to heaven. It's impossible to maintain an uninterrupted spiritual high—no matter how many conferences, Bible camps and book studies you attend. But some churches are so scared of a wildfire that they have no fire. And the deep Christian life isn't a religious roller-coaster ride. Charles Swindoll brings this point home in *Daily Grind*: "You will find people driving miles and miles to attend nightly meetings or standing in long lines to experience some high-level delight that will send them home on the crest of ecstasy. But all this inevitably leads to emotional hangovers." We look for spiritual narcotics to ease the pain of our unfulfilled lives, but they do little more than set us up for crushing periods of doubt and darkness when we no longer "feel something."

RESPONDING TO APATHY

Like just a few drops of food dye will color an entire bowl of water, spiritual apathy will spread to taint every aspect of your life. The only way to escape apathy is to replace it with a fiery passion for holiness.

You can't combat apathy by simply deciding to feel or do something outside of your normal routine. Such resolutions never last. Soon you'll fall back into the same lukewarm state. Willing yourself to "be holy" without allowing God to truly work in your life is like deciding you can jump out of a plane without a parachute—it's unrealistic, dangerous and bound to end badly. In order to eliminate apathy, you must allow God to deal with your self-life. Paul wrote, "So then, my beloved, just as you have always obeyed, not as in my presence only, but now much more in my absence, work out your salvation with fear and trembling; for it is God who is at work in you, both to will and to work for His good pleasure" (Phil. 2:12–13). For God's Word and God's Spirit to operate in your life, you have to cooperate.

It isn't possible to create a holy life in your own strength. If you simply try to maintain your spiritual status, you *will* slip up.

And when you allow yourself to "cool down" enough to accept one night of drinking or looking at pornography or cheating on your spouse, many more will follow. Sin numbs you to righteousness. If God isn't the master of your life, sin will be.

So what do you do with sin? The answer is not to keep rules or retreat to live in a monastery; the answer is found in building a relationship with the Lord through His Word and by His Spirit. It requires dedication to answer the call of Revelation 3:19 to "be zealous and repent." The result is a full life that's on fire for Christ.

Some of us simmer all our lives and never come to a boil. If the fire in your heart has died down, you need to ask the Lord to stir the remaining coals and rekindle the flame. My fear is that those who need to do this the most will remain coolly unconscious of their need and how far away from God they really are. Vance Havner explained that while he was concerned about those who are aware that they need to go to the altar but don't,

> I am more troubled over some who can weather any meeting and sit through countless invitations without ever suspecting that they should have been the first to respond. How many nice, comfortable, lovely people rest smilingly in church pews, their consciences drugged, their wills paralyzed, in a self-satisfied stupor, utterly unconscious of their danger while the Lord of the Lampstands warns them, "I am about to spit you out of my mouth."[6]

G. Campbell Morgan called lukewarmness the worst form of blasphemy. These may sound like strong words, but the truth is that if you aren't fully living for Christ, you're living against Him. If you're putting off what you know He's calling you to do, how can you call yourself a Christ-follower?

Vance Havner was my mentor, so his preaching and writing have highly influenced me. No one addressed the need for personal and corporate revival better than he did. If you can find his book on the churches of Revelation, *Repent or Else,* you owe it to yourself to buy it. He talked about Sunday morning benchwarmers who "traffic in unfelt truth and refuse to get excited over their faith. Their ideal service is a mild-mannered man standing before a group of mild-mannered people exhorting everyone to be more mild-mannered." Does this sound like your experience of church? The good news is that you don't have to settle! Be radical, and actively seek God's best for your life!

You may have just skimmed this section, thinking that it doesn't apply to you because you live a life that's so much *better* than all those hypocrites. Fair enough, but if you turn your gaze inward and are totally honest, I'll bet there's at least one place in which you're being hypocritical. More importantly, it doesn't matter if you're *better* than others. What matters is if you're giving God your *best*.

MAINTAINING PERSPECTIVE

Scientists know that in order to confidently report their findings, the measurements they take during experiments have to be consistent. Using an improperly balanced scale or dirty beaker completely destroys the credibility of the results.

As Christians, we too need to be accurate with our measurements. We can't gauge how hot we are against the temperature of others. Instead we have to determine how spiritually hot or cold we are based on the absolute "thermometer" of the life Christ calls us to in the Bible. The believer who is on fire for God is a thermostat, not a thermometer. They set the temperature; they don't just monitor the temperature currently in the room.

An unfortunately common Christian trend is to get fired up at conferences and in worship at church and then too quickly cool off in between. I heard someone say a long time ago, "It's not how high you jump but how straight you walk when you land."

So how do we live in such a way that we avoid being up and then down, hot and then cold? The key lies in being grounded in the Word. Psalm 119:9 asks and answers an important question: "How can a young man keep his way pure? By keeping it according to Your Word."

Recognizing that he was a poor man without the riches of God's Word, the psalmist wrote, "Your word I have treasured in my heart, that I may not sin against You" (119:11). David knew his heart would follow what he treasured (Matt. 6:21), so he kept God's Word at the center. Because of his humility and correct perspective, David found the Lord's favor.

The psalmist knew the importance of keeping his heart close to the fire of God's Word. Rather than pursuing selfish pleasures and slowly growing cold, he kept his life in God's perspective. He knew that the key to maintaining passion is not making a greater effort to appear holy or doing all the "right things" but rather a daily commitment to the principles, teachings and precepts of God's Word.

No matter how many good things you do, disobedience in even one area will limit your kingdom impact. The truth is not a toy to be played with. The Word of God is given to guide, guard, direct, redirect, correct and teach us the ways of God. The Word gives us insights into what the upgraded life looks like.

You're going to struggle, but when your heart's desire is to walk in step with the Spirit and to trust Him in all things, God's Holy Spirit will guide your steps.

WHICH WAY ARE YOU GOING?

In the field of computers, what was up-to-date in the '90s is irrelevant today. We no longer use floppy discs; now we use flash drives. Very few people use a dial-up modem; now every-thing is wireless and high-speed. When I see Christians who re-fuse to upgrade because they don't want to learn, grow or be stretched, I can hear the grinding sound of a dial-up modem in my head. Those believers might have a connection, but it's weak. They're not as connected to the Spirit as they could be. There's too much sin static in their lives, but they're not doing anything to strengthen the signal. It's almost like they'd rather miss out on God's blessings than give up the sins slowing down their development.

Just as I can't imagine anyone longing to return to the days of dial-up, I don't understand why believers think it's okay to tolerate sins that separate them from God. Our response to sin should never be a halfhearted, "Oops, guess I shouldn't have done that." Sin distances us from our holy God, so we should abhor every hint of it in our lives. Donald Grey Barnhouse writes, "If sin comes into the life of the believer, he should im-mediately become concerned about it. It should cause him to rush to the Lord in confession and repentance, and it should cause him to build every bulwark possible against the recur-rence of the sin."

If you can sin or casually watch others sin without being af-fected, you've lost touch with the heart of God. Being in God's will requires an understanding of moral absolutes. When you hate something, you want to avoid it at all costs. The best way to minimize your sinful nature is to pray like the psalmist that the Lord might have control over your heart: "Direct my footsteps according to Your Word; let no sin rule over me" (119:133, NIV).

One of the most common images used in Psalm 119 is a path, which refers to a life direction.

"Before I was afflicted I went astray [took the wrong path], but now I keep Your word." (119:67)

"I have restrained my feet from every evil way [path], that I may keep Your word." (119:101)

"I hate every false path." (119:104, NIV)

"Your word is a lamp to my feet and a light to my path." (119:105)

"Because I consider all your precepts right, I hate every wrong path." (119:125, NIV)

God's Word is our road map. As long as we follow it, we're fine. The lamp and light of the Word will keep us from detours and potholes that can get us off track or out of alignment with the Spirit. But as soon as we start following the opinions and reasoning of men, we start down wrong side paths, which eventually lead us to spiritual dead ends.

Men are notorious for not asking for directions. I am directionally dysfunctional. I have to look at my car's digital compass to know which direction I'm going. A few weeks ago, my navigation system went haywire. Even though I knew where I was going, I had turned on my GPS to check travel times. It (or she, since mine has the voice of a British woman) tried to get me to take every exit off the interstate. I finally had to turn the thing off because it was leading me off the road I knew I was supposed to be on. Later I took the car to the shop and had a new navigation system installed. If I had listened to the GPS on that trip, I probably would have ended up in the middle of nowhere, halfexpecting some awful creature to emerge from the swamp and swallow me whole.

Similarly, if you refuse to follow the map God has laid out for you in His Word, you'll end up in the wrong place. You might be on a dark, winding back road, or you might be on a wide, beautifully paved road—either way you'll be headed the wrong direction. If you don't follow the narrow road Scripture talks about, you'll end up wasting time, if not your whole life.

I've counseled people throughout my ministry who have gotten off track and wasted their lives. They wouldn't listen to counsel because they wanted to be in control. They thought they knew better than God. The end results of such disobedience are always sin, pain and regret.

When you sin, you willingly step off the straight and narrow path that is eternal life in Christ. Once you've done this, you only have one option: turn around and go back to wherever you got off track. And remember, the farther down the wrong road you go, the longer it will take you to get back on track. Take time now to pray Psalm 119:10: "With all my heart I have sought You; do not let me wander from Your commandments." When you are set on obeying the Word, the Holy Spirit will lead and guide you down the correct path.

Being on Fire for God . . . with God!

"Do you have just enough religion to make you decent, but not enough to make you dynamic?" Vance Havner once asked. Being dynamic or "on fire" in your Christian walk starts with maintaining an intimate relationship with the Lord. Your spiritual temperature is a good indicator of where you put God in your life. He longs to be in a *personal* relationship with you.

Think about when you first fell in love. Remember your desire to spend as much time as possible with that person and to do anything possible to please him or her? Your relationship with your Creator should be like that—only entirely honest and permanent.

Through the Holy Spirit you have access to God who loves you in a personal way and who wants you to be wholly His. Look at how David addressed the Lord in Psalm 119. He used intimate language and mentioned God's name in every verse. The psalmist referred to himself 325 times with personal pronouns like "I," "my," "me," "mine," "myself" and "your servant."

Although Psalm 119 mentions God's law, David didn't ask for a legalistic presentation of how to keep the rules. Rather than maintaining a list of dos and don'ts, David desired to be instructed by the Lord and asked for strength to keep the Word. Uninterested in a transitory faith, he worked on building a strong relationship with God.

God created you in His image, and He knows you intimately. Do you have the desire to be close to Him? Read the following verses from Psalm 119, and take note of repeated words and of the attributes of God highlighted by the psalmist.

"Remove the false way from me, and graciously grant me Your law." (119:29)

"Establish Your word to Your servant, as that which produces reverence for You." (119:38)

"May Your lovingkindnesses also come to me, O LORD, Your salvation according to Your word." (119:41)

"I shall delight in Your commandments, which I love. And I shall lift up my hands to Your commandments, which I love." (119:47–48)

"I sought Your favor with all my heart; be gracious to me according to Your word." (119:58)

"O may Your lovingkindnesses comfort me, according to Your word to Your servant. May Your compassion come to me that I may live, for Your law is my delight." (119:76–77)

"Turn to me and be gracious to me, after Your manner with those who love Your name." (119:132)

"Great are Your mercies, O LORD; revive me according to Your ordinances." (119:156)

What words jumped out at you? David appealed to God's graciousness, compassion, greatness and lawfulness. David delighted in the law of the God of mercy and love and came before the One he loved in reverence.

What does your relationship with God look like? Have you fully invested in Him, seeking to know Him and to follow His commands, or do you simply wave at Him on Sunday mornings and avoid Him the rest of the week?

Real relationships require investment. God is worthy of all your adoration, so stop settling for only giving Him part of what He deserves. Remember: the best way to stay enthusiastically dedicated to and "on fire" for God is to stay close to Him—the source of the flame!

KNOWING AND ACTING ON THE WORD

God loves you, so He isn't going to allow you to flounder, wondering what a close relationship with Him might look like. The Bible is the inspired Word of God, and it tells us what the Lord has said and how we are to act in light of it. Following its guidelines is the best way to avoid the cooling off of false religiosity. God's Word is clear, and when God speaks, He doesn't stutter or beat around the bush.

"Torah" (the name for the first five books of the Old Testament) is derived from the Hebrew word meaning "to direct, to guide, to instruct." God's will is revealed in His Word, and it sums up the expectations for our obedience. It isn't enough to *know* the Lord's laws; you also have to *follow* them. The upgraded life is committed to knowing and doing.

Following the Lord's law allows us to access His promises. His Word lays out the way we are to navigate this life. Think of it as a road map, a course of action spelled out in writing.

God's directions come in several forms. There are *mispatim*, ordinances or rulings; commandments, orders issued with authority; statutes, prescribed, written law; and *piqqudim*, precepts or charges. *Piqqudim* means "to place in trust." God's laws have been entrusted to us, so we're responsible to heed them.

Christians are not only supposed to know the law; we're called to both live according to the law and to share its truths with others. The Pharisees knew the Law, and they could quote books of the Bible. But their hearts were hardened and cold, and they opposed the very Son of God standing in their midst. That's why the Scriptures talk about "Spirit and truth." We need both. Lost people can be religious and know facts about the Bible, but they have no power to live it out.

God's word is meant to be proclaimed. In Hebrew, the word for "word" is *dabar*, and it carries the connotation of being set forth in speech. The verb *hedot* means "to bear witness" or "to testify." When people are transformed by the Lord, they want to tell others of His good and perfect law, sharing the effect it has had on their lives.

Do you frequently share about what God has done in your life? D. Martyn Lloyd-Jones writes, "At the final bar of judgment the gravest charge that will be made against us Christians will be that we were so unconcerned." If you love the Lord, you'll care about His world, and if you care about His world, you'll make an effort to share His love with others. This is a biblical command!

At the church I pastor, we recently embarked on the most aggressive mission effort in our sixty-year history. The scope is global. We are committed to reaching our community (Jerusalem), our region (Judea), our nation (Samaria) and the uttermost parts of the earth. Why? The Word gives us a Great Commission. We recognize that in order to receive God's blessings as a church, we have to be obedient. God's Word calls us to care and share. No matter your theological slant, the command to care for this world and share the good news is not optional for believers.

God's laws are established in order to govern us and to keep us on the correct path, and He holds us accountable to follow them. The Word of God keeps us from dabbling in secondary things and causes us to focus on God's agenda. There's a world of difference between a good idea and a God idea. God has not called us to imitate others. Imitation is not the key. Incarnation is the key—"Christ *in* you." Since rules require reinforcement and God is a righteous judge, He pays attention to the way we respond to His mandates.

Have you resolved to follow God's Word—no matter how strong the opposition? Verses like Psalm 119: 67, 71 and 75 reveal to us that even though David faced affliction, he trusted the Lord. Staying on fire for God involves knowing His commands, obeying His Word, and trusting that He will be faithful to guide your steps.

REAL TRANSFORMATION

It's not enough to admit that you need to change or to say, "I need to make an adjustment." Talk all you want, real transformation only comes when you take steps to alter your situation by taking God at His Word and depending on the Holy Spirit. The psalmist wasn't content to live a mediocre faith. Are you?

David got honest before the living God; this is what J.I. Packer refers to as "spiritual realism." The psalms reflect David's desire to know as much of God as possible. He blended head knowledge of the Word with a heart experience of the living God. He wasn't content to maintain the middle ground in his faith; instead, he recognized there's always more to learn and do.

Even when David was going through a trying season, he coupled his reflections on the situation with God's truths. Read these verses from Psalm 119:

"My soul cleaves to the dust; revive me according to Your word." (119:25)

"My soul weeps because of grief; strengthen me according to Your word." (119:28)

"This is my comfort in my affliction, that Your word has revived me." (119:50)

Through every difficulty David turned to the Bible. But then in verse 82 he noted, "My eyes fail . . . for Your word" (119:82). Don't think that the Bible is a magic book or a wish book. Sometimes the Word doesn't have the answers you want, but it has the answers you need. Don't give up on God's Word. Stay in it. Read it until you see it and believe it. It's true—even when you can't see or feel God working in the moment.

Take the living God at His Word. His promises are yes and amen. Even when it didn't seem to be helping and he didn't seem to be getting anything out of it, David kept searching the Scriptures. Reading the Bible can be like brushing your teeth; it's good whether you can see the direct effects now or not, and it keeps you from falling into decay. What you read today can bless you tomorrow. God's Word is true, and you need it to stay close to the Lord—through *every* situation.

I'm always surprised when people drop out of church when they hit hard times. It's through life's difficulties that you need people to understand what you're going through and to pray for and support you. (But if you only go to church to use God as a quick fix for your problems and to get an emotional high, your faith is cold.) Don't give up when you hit a dry spell!

In Psalm 119:83 David wrote, "Though I have become like a wineskin in the smoke, I do not forget Your statutes." In David's day wine was often stored in leather bags, and if the leather was left out in the sun long enough, it would dry out, get hard and crack. It was no longer able to perform its proper function of holding liquid. In other words, David was spent and was running on empty, but take note of the second half of that verse: "I do not forget Your statues." Even though he felt dry, David remembered the law of the Lord.

David proclaimed, "If Your law had not been my delight, then I would have perished in my affliction" (119:92). Strength to overcome your situation is not in your own abilities; it is in the cleansing truth of the Word of God and the empowerment of the Holy Spirit. Steadfast trust, honest self-evaluation and ardent Scripture-searching are required for maintaining spiritual heat.

Are you willing to put your faith in what God has said? Are you ready to not just believe *in* Him but to *believe Him* for everything He's said He's going to do in your life? You won't experience His full power until you let go of notions of your own strength.

Don't settle for mediocrity. Allow God to change you now, and then do what He has commanded! One of my heroes, Manley Beasley, used to say, "Faith is believing that it's so when it's not so, so it can be so because God said so."

ACTING ON THE PROMISES

Are you enthusiastic about what God is doing in your life? The word "enthusiasm" comes from two Greek words—*en*, meaning "in," and *theos*, meaning "God." In other words, true enthusiasm springs from being close to God. And when the Lord is at work in your life and you're seeking more of His presence, your faith won't have a chance to grow cold.

Having God close to your heart will give you a fresh perspective. The psalmist looked at the world around him, and his heart was broken: "Streams of tears flow from my eyes, for Your law is not obeyed" (119:136).

What do you see when you observe your environment? Many Christians allow their motives to be distorted by the world's priorities, the opinion of others, or even other carnal Christians who don't want to pay the price for an upgrade. But in order to be righteous, you have to reject everything that even gives an inkling of corruption.

If you look at the example of David, you see that he hated everything that was not of God. He asked the Lord, "Redeem me from the oppression of man, that I may keep Your precepts" (119:134). In Psalm 119:113 he told God that he couldn't stand being around people who said one thing and did another: "I hate those who are double-minded, but I love Your law." It's not just that David mildly disliked being with those who didn't follow God's law; he wanted nothing to do with them: "Depart from me, evildoers, that I may observe the commandments of my God" (119:115). David's response to corruption was not to turn a blind eye and peaceably keep to himself; instead he passionately desired change: "Burning indignation has seized me because of the wicked, who forsake Your law" (119:53).

When's the last time you wept over lawless culture? In Psalm 119:136 David exclaimed, "My eyes shed streams of water, because they do not keep Your law." David had the correct understanding of sin and wickedness—he abhorred them: "My zeal has consumed me, because my adversaries have forgotten Your words. . . . I behold the treacherous and loathe them, because they do not keep Your word" (119: 139, 158).

What makes God angry should make you angry. So what exactly does God detest? Look at Romans, in which God gives those who have turned their back on Him over to their desires:

> Just as they did not see fit to acknowledge God any longer, God gave them over to a depraved mind, to do those things which are not proper, being filled with all unrighteousness, wickedness, greed, evil; full of envy, murder, strife, deceit, malice; they are gossips, slanderers, haters of God, insolent, arrogant, boastful, inventors of evil, disobedient to parents, without understanding, untrustworthy, unloving, unmerciful; and although they know the ordinance of God, that those who practice such things are worthy of death, they not only do the same, but also give hearty approval to those who practice them. (1:28–32)

This passage is not simply about the evils of a pagan culture. Some of these same practices were (and still are) in the church, and they make God sick!

As I work on this chapter, I've just finished reading my friend Andy Andrews's book *How Do You Kill 11 Million People? Why the Truth Matters More than You Think*. It's one of the most powerful books I've ever read. In the book he deals with what happens to a nation when we stop caring, start believing lies and refuse to stand for truth. It reminded me that the statement of Jesus—"You will know the truth, and the truth will make you free" (John 8:32)—is one of the most pivotal statements in the Word and in human history.

But, you might ask, isn't sin natural? Yes, you're born with a natural inclination to sin, but you still *choose* to do it. The reality is that you are God's child, yet you choose to disobey His laws. You choose to ignore His truth. Sin wouldn't be sin if you didn't have any choice in the matter because you could simply lay the blame on someone or something else. Dr. Chris Wright notes, "That is why we have so little repentance and so little forgiveness. When you reduce a person's responsibility, you remove the very first opportunity they have to step back toward repentance and forgiveness and grace."[7]

Reading Psalm 119, we see David's deliberate act of will in choosing not to sin. In verse 110 he explained, "I have kept my feet from every evil path so that I might obey Your word." David longed to live in accordance with God's Word at all times—not just when the going was easy. He reaffirmed his commitment for the long haul in verses 106 and 112: "I have taken an oath and confirmed it. . . . My heart is set on keeping Your decrees to the very end."

You have to make a stand now for what you believe, or you'll easily be swept into an "anything goes" mentality. Workers, don't settle for an inappropriate work environment; if Christ would rebuke it, so should you. Mothers and wives, it should grieve you if your husband and children dismiss God's Word. Church member, don't settle for a dead church where the truth is not proclaimed in power. (I don't care if your grandmother was a charter member and was buried in your church's cemetery. You owe no loyalty to any organization that has left its roots and forgotten its heritage. You owe no loyalty to a preacher, teacher or church that has forsaken the truth.)

God didn't give His Son for us to have opinions but for us to live by convictions. Retaining your fire for the Lord requires wholehearted commitment to His Word.

AN HONEST EVALUATION

So where are you today? Perhaps you're aware that your faith has grown cold or perhaps you've never made a commitment to fully live for God.

Your spiritual temperature isn't measured by how many Bible studies you attend or by how many Christians are in your family; it's measured by the extent of your love and dedication to the Lord. Don't take a backseat in your life, allowing apathy to grow until it's the only thing that defines you. Christ has called you to a bold, impassioned faith.

Manley Beasley suggested that you take a jug of water and your Bible into the woods and stay there until you meet God. That's not a bad idea. If you want to go deeper with God, it's going to demand a serious adjustment on your part.

If you're struggling with lukewarmness, get in the Word. Talk to God in prayer. Be the flame in a mediocre environment.

God desires for each of us to radically seek and follow Him. Never say no to His leading. Instead, ask Him to burn away everything that is not of Him in your life and to set a fire in your heart to passionately live for Him. Don't settle for yesterday's "good enough"; strive for God's best for you each day. It's time to upgrade your life.

Grieving the Holy Spirit

'M A CHILD of the '60s, and I grew up watching the *Dick Van Dyke Show*. There's a continuing joke in the show's opening sequence that always makes me laugh. When Dick walks through his front door, he sees his house full of friends. When he tries to walk over to them, he trips over a footstool and falls. The same thing happens every time. I've always wondered—why didn't he move the stool?

We're a lot like Dick Van Dyke—we're always tripping over things. Rather than dealing with the obstacles and attitudes that impede our lives, we keep functioning in the same ways, allowing the same problems to mess us up time and time again. We run to the altar, but we don't allow it to alter our lives after we leave the church. We decide to turn over a new leaf and voice our recommitment—but somehow we fail to follow through.

We become accustomed to living in a subpar fashion. Footstools, or "little" sins, become commonplace. And worse, we justify our continual tripping and falling. Giving into temptation becomes the rule rather than the exception.

Look at the news. Robberies, vandalism and even murders are reported so frequently that we've become dull to the shock of hearing about them. We've lost our ability to blush in seeing man's inhumanity to man. Pictures that once horrified us now flash before our eyes as we eat popcorn. Nothing surprises us. We are numb to the news and accustomed to tragedy. We tend to push issues to the back of our minds. *That's not* my *problem*, we think.

We almost stop noticing the stories—until, that is, something happens to someone famous. We all know about the murders of men like JFK and Martin Luther King Jr. because of the impact those crimes had on society. We all heard about Bill Clinton's affair, and we're all aware of the offenses of professional athletes. Murder is murder, but if someone who is significant in the eyes of society gets killed, the coverage given to the story is much greater. Intentionally or not, we tend to judge the enormity of a crime by the importance of the victim.

We might scream in outrage when others get away with major crimes against figureheads we follow. But do we react the same when we're the ones at fault? When we look into the mirror, do we see liars, thieves and murderers staring back at us?

We go about our days tripping over the footstools of sin and not recognizing that we're guilty of serious crimes against a significant Person. If spiritual sins were reported on the nightly news, many of us would be featured for atrocious acts against a major personality. But many of us don't even know who we're injuring by our actions.

WHO ARE WE HURTING?

Do you ever wonder why so many Christians seem to lack joy in their lives? Ever wonder why the people in the pews aren't victorious? The number one reason Christians fail to walk in Christ's triumph is that they have grieved the Holy Ghost.

We have become so jaded and insensitive that we're unaware we're grieving the third member of the Trinity by our words and actions. It's hard to accept that any believer would betray the One who lives in us, teaches us and prays for us. But the fact is that the Spirit who was present at creation and at the resurrection is grieved by the way many of us live our lives.

Ephesians 4:30 clearly states, "Do not grieve the Holy Spirit of God." We need to solemnly consider this command because the Bible doesn't give us irrelevant instruction. God never wastes words or thoughts.

The word "grieve" suggests the presence of love. It's possible to be angry or irritated with a stranger, but you aren't really grieved by others' actions unless you truly care about them. You can only emotionally hurt someone who loves you. By acting and responding in ways that are not consistent with the character of the Holy Spirit, believers cause Him great pain and sorrow.

As a pastor, I've learned a great deal about human nature and am convinced that the majority of Christians' problems today stem from issues of the heart. Selfless, generous love does not come naturally to us, and living in a self-centered, fallen manner is dangerous. We can't afford to ostracize the Holy Spirit, because He is our comforter as well as our prayer partner who intercedes for us. We need His guidance to enjoy an upgraded Christian life! As John Wesley notes, "Without the Spirit of God we can do nothing but add sin to sin."[8]

By examining the specifics of how we grieve the Spirit, we can find positive ways to cultivate His presence in our lives and to maintain an intimate relationship with Him. Ephesians calls us to "speak truth" (4:25) and to "let all bitterness and wrath and anger and clamor and slander be put away from you, along with all malice. Be kind to one another, tender-hearted, for-giving each other, just as God in Christ also has forgiven you" (4:31–32). These verses refer to the kind of attitudes we should exemplify as believers—evidence of a Spirit-controlled life that is counter to the selfish impulses that wound the Spirit.

If you're currently struggling to live in the joy of the Lord, it's probably because you've done something to grieve the Spirit. Are you willing to take the necessary steps to repair your fellow-ship with Him?

STOP THE DECEPTION!

It's impossible to sin without reaping consequences. In other words, when you sin—in your heart and with your actions—it has a negative effect on you and those around you. Grieving the Spirit puts to death (or at the least quenches) His work in your life and hinders Him from producing in you the fruit of the Spirit—love, joy, peace, patience, kindness, goodness, faithful-ness, gentleness and self-control. You become unable to grow in your faith, and you lose the joy of your salvation.

Are you wondering whether or not you've truly been saved? First John 3:24 says, "The one who keeps [God's] command-ments abides in Him, and He in him. We know by this that He abides in us, by the Spirit whom He has given us." One ministry of the Holy Spirit is to assure you of your salvation. If you're struggling and doubting your salvation, you need to reevaluate whether or not you are walking in the Spirit. All the evidences of salvation mentioned in First John are in the present tense. Salvation is more than a decision made in the past; it includes evidence of that decision in the present. If there's no fruit in your life, you need to seriously ask yourself if you're rooted and grounded in Christ—and the Holy Spirit will help you answer that question.

When's the last time you honestly evaluated your Christian walk? Are you truly living in a godly fashion, or are you poking the leftover embers of a flame that once burned brightly for the Lord? Are you justifying a mediocre, joyless faith, even though it contradicts the instruction of the Holy Spirit? Deceiving yourself into believing you're following the Lord when you aren't is sin.

First Samuel tells the story of Israel's first king, Saul, who reaped the consequences of his deception. In 15:3 the Lord instructed Samuel to destroy *all* the Amalekites and *all* their livestock and goods, but after his army took the city of Amalek, Saul spared King Agag and all the best animals. When Saul reported back to Samuel, he spoke in half-truths saying, "I have carried out the command of the Lord" (15:13), and "I did obey the voice of the Lord" (15:20).

Saul rationalized his actions by claiming he had spared the choice animals to sacrifice to God, but he knew he had failed to follow the Lord's instruction and had ignored Samuel's authority. Because he disobeyed God's command, Saul lost his divine anointing.

Saul pretended to be more spiritual than he was, and it got him in trouble and caused him to miss out on the Lord's blessing. Does this ever sound like you? You do *some* things for God but ignore the things you aren't doing for Him—and you still claim you're fully obeying Him. I heard a preacher say years ago, "Partial obedience is total disobedience."

Don't allow what happened to Saul to happen to you. Do an honest evaluation of your life. God knows the areas in which you struggle to follow Him, and He has sent His Holy Spirit to give you the strength to obey His commands. But in order to have access to the Spirit, you have to commit to honestly following 100 percent of what the Lord asks of you.

Do God's Will God's Way

Saul's main problem was that he set himself against the revealed will of God. His sin was willful. He destroyed only what he wanted to destroy. He was driven by greed and vanity rather than by a desire to listen to God's command.

The Amalekites are symbolic of a fleshly, self-gratifying, fallen nature. Failing to destroy them meant condoning what God condemned. God doesn't bargain. You can't play "Let's Make a Deal" with Him. When you place convenience above conviction, you increase the stronghold of self-pride over your life and set yourself up for a costly fall.

Saul was a rebellious compromiser. He tried to appear holy while striving for worldly commendation. I see this attitude every Sunday. People wear their best clothes and act like they love Jesus, but if you saw them getting ready and driving to church, you'd wonder if they were saved. There's more pretending in the average Sunday morning crowd than any of us would care to admit. Unfortunately, churchgoers are often unwilling to admit their shortcomings in front of other believers—fearing they'll be regarded as inferior. But the truth is that we're all sinners, and our cover-ups don't work.

Verse 24 tells us that Saul "feared the people and listened to their voice." He was more worried about what his peers thought than what God commanded. When confronted with his sin, Saul thought of his reputation rather than his need to repent. In verse 15:30 he said, "I have sinned; but please honor me now before the elders of my people and before Israel, and go back with me, that I may worship the Lord your God." Do you see how this is more of a plea for praise than for righteousness?

Saul's actions wrought eternal consequences. Verse 35 states, "The Lord regretted He made Saul king." This doesn't mean God had made a mistake nor that He had changed His mind about

Saul; rather, it means He was grieved by Saul's failure and all of his missed potential.

Ignoring God's Word and trying to live on our own terms always leads to trouble. We may not fully see the consequences of our disobedience, but it can destroy our witness, our trustworthiness and our relationships, including with the Lord. Disobeying God's Word and then trying to justify it grieves the Holy Spirit.

IT'S NOT MY FAULT!

When you accept that your relationship with God isn't what it should be, your first reaction is often to find someone or something to blame. You might lament, "If only I hadn't been raised this way . . ." or "Maybe if my pastor was a better preacher . . ." These justifications may make sense to you in the moment, but what happens when you examine them against biblical teachings?

Saul's excuses didn't get him very far. Even though he had been given clear direction from the Lord, he didn't do what God said. Rather than owning up and admitting that what he had done was wrong, he tried to spin the situation to make himself sound right and holy. When Samuel confronted Saul and asked, "Why then did you not obey the voice of the Lord, but rushed upon the spoil and did what was evil in the sight of the Lord?" (15:19), Saul deceitfully replied, "I did obey the voice of the Lord." (15:20).

Samuel wasn't about to take Saul's weak lie. Samuel knew the importance of thoroughly following God's will, so he replied,

> Has the Lord as much delight in burnt offerings and sacrifices as in obeying the voice of the Lord? Behold, to obey is better than sacrifice and to heed than the fat of rams. For rebellion is as the sin of divination, and insubordination is as iniquity and idolatry. Because you have rejected the word of the Lord, He has also rejected you from being king. (15:22–23)

This may seem like a harsh punishment, but Saul needed to be broken out of his rebellion and stubbornness. His actions—however "correct" he deemed them—contradicted God's design. First John 2:3–4 tells us, "The one who says, 'I have come to know Him,' and does not keep His commandments, is a liar, and the truth is not in him." In order to know God and His purpose for our lives, we have to obey Him!

Saul convinced himself he had a better plan than the Lord, and it led to his downfall. Don't be like Saul. Commit to honestly admitting your errors, and strive to honor God's commands.

STEPS TO SPIRITUAL FREEDOM

Ephesians 4:25–30 tells us to lay aside falsehood and speak truth, to exchange unwholesome words for well-timed words of edification and to put away bitterness and anger in favor of kindness and forgiveness.

If you follow what Paul said in these verses, you'll save yourself from heading down the wrong path. If you disregard his words of wisdom, you'll grieve the Holy Spirit, which will cut you off from the blessing of the fullness of life in Christ.

1) *Love others.* Without exception, everything Paul mentioned in these verses in Ephesians has to do with relationships with others. Unless you live in a bubble, you're going to have to deal with people, and how you interact with others determines where you stand in your relationship with the Lord. God is serious about how we live, what we say, how we think and how we respond to others.

2) *Don't lie.* We live in a culture that thrives on deception. Advertisements, politicians and the media tell us so many half-truths that we get used to hearing lies, but Paul forbade lying. Why? There are no innocent, little white lies. Telling half-truths makes your soul rot away. When you lie, you grieve the Spirit

and cut Him off from working in your life (John 15:26). Paul saw lying as a dominant characteristic of the old, Spirit-grieving life. Rather than denouncing lying as a sin against God, Paul dealt with it as a sin against the body of Christ: "Do not lie to one another" (Col. 3:9).

Verse 22 tells us to "lay aside the old self, which is being corrupted in accordance with the lusts of deceit." John Phillips writes, "The old man has deceitful desires that produce corruption in him just as putrefaction produces corruption in a corpse. There is nothing attractive about a decaying carcass; it fills us with horror and disgust. Its corruption is most offensive. Nobody would want to share life with a corpse."[9]

So what's the alternative? Paul went on to command us to "put on the new self" and "be renewed in the spirit of your mind" (4: 24–23). This trading of the old man for the new signifies a move from deceit to holiness. When your mind is renewed, you see people through God's perspective. When truth fills your life, others will see the fruit of the Spirit (Gal. 5:22) in you.

3) *Don't be angry.* Paul says, "Be angry, and yet do not sin" (4:26). Frederick Buechner offers good insight on the result of anger:

> Of the seven deadly sins, anger is possibly the most fun. To lick your wounds, to smack your lips over grievances long past, to roll over your tongue the prospect of bitter confrontation still to come, to savor to the last toothsome morsel both the pain you are given and the pain you are giving back; in many ways it is a feast fit for a king. The chief drawback is that what you are wolfing down is yourself. The skeleton at the feast is you.[10]

Just because you aren't yelling at people doesn't mean you aren't allowing the devil to have a foothold of bitterness in your heart. Anger doesn't just beat down those around you; it also eats away at you from within.

But sin should make us angry. Jesus was filled with righteous anger when He cleansed the temple (read Mark 11:15–18), and we should be righteously angry over the sins of society and when people pervert doctrinal truths. However, it's important to be angry at the right things for the right reasons and to remain in control over our thoughts and our tongue.

4) *Don't steal.* This command of Paul might surprise you. *Wait,* you might think, *isn't he writing to Christians?* Yes, he is. There are members of churches who take things that don't belong to them. Theft is broader than walking out of a store with unpaid merchandise under your shirt. Lying on income taxes, borrowing and not returning something from an acquaintance, using office time to make personal calls and keeping the Lord's tithe for yourself are all examples of stealing.

Paul's answer to theft is simple yet challenging. He urged us to labor so that we "have something to share with one who has need" (4:28). In other words, rather than always looking to see what you can get out of a situation, work hard and honestly and strive to be a giver.

5) *Speak encouragement.* Paul cautioned, "Let no unwholesome word proceed from your mouth" (4:29). "Unwholesome" means bad, rotten and filthy. It's the same word that might be used to describe a decaying animal or rotten vegetable. Unwholesome talk includes obscene language, but Paul emphasized not speaking in ways that run others down or increase their misfortune. To keep from grieving the Spirit, watch your mouth! Speak edifying words that build others up and encourage them in their walk with Christ.

6) *Forgive.* Paul started Ephesians 4:31 by commanding us to put away bitterness. He then condemned wrath, anger, clamor, slander and malice. Do you see the progression? It starts with bitterness, and it ends with "malice," which is the Greek term for

"depravity." When you're spiteful—having a mean-spirited disposition that gets a kick out of seeing bad things happen to people you don't like—you're sinning. This attitude of resentment festers beneath the surface, and when it finally bursts forth, it has devastating effects. (For example, church splits often originate in one person's evil words about a brother or sister in Christ.)

If you want to walk in the freedom of the Spirit, you have to surrender your hurts. You have the power to forgive because God forgave you. Verse 32 exhorts us, "Be kind to one another, tender-hearted, forgiving each other, just as God in Christ also has forgiven you." Even though forgiveness is difficult, it frees you from negative feelings that can grow and corrupt your heart.

Struggling to get over something from your past or to forgive someone is a sign you haven't fully yielded yourself to the Lord, and this grieves the Spirit. Stop pointing fingers and making excuses. Leave the judging up to God, and live in His freedom!

HOW WILL YOU END UP?

Saul never saw Samuel again after the confrontation. Similarly, if you insist on continuing in a sinful lifestyle, there will be a day when God will leave you to the consequences of your decisions and actions. Hebrews 10:26 tells us, "For if we go on sinning willfully after receiving the knowledge of the truth, there no longer remains a sacrifice for sins."

You don't want God to fall silent. Saul's life ended tragically. He turned to witchcraft and consulting mediums and eventually committed suicide. Ironically, the end of a king who refused to be humbled was lowly and disgraceful. Because he rejected the Word of God, God rejected him.

But there is hope, and it comes through abandonment to the Lord Jesus Christ. We should pray like William Culberson, "Lord, help us end well."

You've seen how Saul's deception grieved God and got him in trouble, and you've read Paul's advice on how loving others in the body will keep you from distancing yourself from the Spirit. Now the question is—what are you going to do with this information?

The simple way to keep from grieving the Spirit is to continually seek more of Him in your life. To avoid tripping over sin, follow God's commands and claim His promises.

Jesus (and only Jesus) has the power to save us from ourselves. Through His sacrifice, He has given us the ability and resources to say along with Paul in Romans 7:24–25, "Wretched man that I am! Who will set me free from the body of this death? Thanks be to God—through Jesus Christ our Lord!"

Just as you defragment your computer to rid the system of excess and junk, allow the Holy Spirit to wipe your heart clean. Don't keep visiting the sites of your past sin. Instead, daily commit yourself to Christ's lordship. Be filled with the Spirit, and allow Him to set you free.

II

YOUR UPGRADE IS READY

Stop Wandering! Recognize God's Promises

EVERY MEMBER of my family has an iPhone 4. Two of them even have the 4S. Because I don't qualify for an upgrade, I'm still using my Blackberry. When the time comes for an upgrade, I may go to the iPhone, but the truth is that I prefer feeling the keys to tapping on a screen. (I know—I'm pretty old school.) The iPhone has many features and apps I would enjoy, but I have to ask myself, is it worth it? I've been using a Blackberry for so long I'm not sure I really want to take the time to learn a whole new system.

Think about what I've just said. When you boil it down, I don't want to upgrade. I'm not sure I want to pay the price to have a more efficient way of doing things. It's hard because every time a new Apple product releases, the hype gets bigger and the line outside the store gets longer. When the iPad 2 came out, it sold out—around 500,000 units—in less than a day![11] Those who missed out on buying one the first day had to wait weeks in some places to get their hands on one of the gadgets. The same thing happened with the iPhone 4S. It's crazy how addicted we are to the latest technology.

Let's bring this discussion a little closer to home. Is there a book series you like reading, a recording artist you enjoy listening to or a video game you enjoy playing? Recently, cult followings have formed around the *Harry Potter* and *Twilight* series, and I myself always anticipate John Grisham's next novel. Sherwood Pictures starts getting e-mails right after a new movie releases asking about our next project. (Those e-mails and questions make me wonder if anyone understands the work and cost to make a feature film!) My favorite Christian author is Warren Wiersbe, and I look forward to reading what he has to say in each new book. What about you? Do you ever count down the days until a new release, anxiously wondering what your experience with a new product will be like?

As excited as you are for the latest and greatest manufactured good, you should be one thousand times more passionate about the life upgrade available in Christ. This upgrade is available 24/7. There's no waiting list. This upgrade doesn't need fancy packaging or marketing hype because it's offering something truly amazing—*victory*. So why isn't everyone clamoring to get it?

The term "victorious Christian life" can be misleading because it sounds as if it's some special form of Christianity, when in reality it's *the* Christian life. Because Christ took our sins upon Himself, we share in His glorious victory. Being a victorious Christian doesn't mean you're never going to sin—it just means you're continuously learning to depend on Christ.

Walking in victory is challenging. It involves daily sacrifice and a dedication to stand firm on God's promises. Here's the thing—the more you give to God, the more He'll require of you. But that's a positive thing because He works everything for your good (Rom. 8:28). To enjoy an upgraded Christian life, you have to trust the Creator, believe the promises of the Word of God and depend on the Holy Spirit.

BELIEVING GOD'S PROMISES

The Old Testament character Joshua is a strong example of a man who obeyed God's commands and trusted His Word. We can learn a lot from his dedication to trust the Lord through thick and thin. In order to grasp the depths of Joshua's reliance on the Lord, we first have to understand his culture.

Exodus, Leviticus, Numbers and Deuteronomy tell the story of the Israelites' forty years of wandering in the desert. After decades passed and millions of the sojourners' relatives died, Moses gave a final charge. He (1) commanded the people to obey God and follow Him, (2) reminded the people of God's provision and promise, saying, "The LORD is the one who goes ahead of you; He will be with you. He will not fail you or forsake you" (Deut. 31:8) and (3) organized the people to move on under Joshua's leadership. Moses encouraged the new generation of desert-wanderers to trust God's promises for the present and future rather than to long for a lost past. Basically, Moses was saying, "We've lived long enough in the wilderness. Your ancestors rejected the possibility of an upgrade and lost the Promised Land. I'm putting before you the possibility of an upgraded life in a land flowing with milk and honey. It will require a learning curve, but it's worth it."

Moses was a tough act to follow, but God didn't call Joshua to be another Moses. God called Joshua to follow Him. The name Joshua means "Jehovah, the Savior," so it's important to remember that the key figure in Joshua isn't actually Joshua—it's God. Joshua arrived on the scene during a period of serious transition and uncertainty, but he recognized it wasn't up to him to "fix" anything. He just had to trust the Lord to make good on

His promise that the Israelites' wandering in the desert was coming to an end. The people were to leave behind the old baggage of disobedience and unbelief and cross over into the Promised Land. God promised to upgrade them from just enough manna for each day to a land flowing with milk and honey. That's a serious upgrade—like going from the early days of cell phones the size of a milk carton to the ones we have today that fit in your pocket. Why would anyone turn that down?

The Israelites had to wait a *long* time before they were ready to enter the Promised Land. God didn't hand them His blessings on a silver platter. In the same way, we have to be equipped to accept our upgrade.

BEING PREPARED FOR AN UPGRADE

You can't wake up one morning and decide to be an entirely different person by that same afternoon. Receiving an upgrade in Christ requires trusting in Him and relying on His timing. In the Israelites' case this meant waiting for an entire unfaithful generation to pass. It was only after Moses's death that the Lord raised up Joshua to lead His people to their upgrade. And even then, Joshua had to face some difficulties.

Joshua 1:1 starts on a dark note: "Now it came about after the death of Moses the servant of the Lord that the Lord spoke to Joshua the son of Nun, Moses's servant, saying, 'Moses My servant is dead.'" Although Joshua knew he'd eventually have to face that day, he must have been stunned. "Moses is dead. Now, Joshua, you must lead. The baton has been passed." If you've ever been in a hospital room when someone is pronounced dead, you know the sickening feeling that washes over you and makes your heart drop. But imagine if you knew that you had to take over that person's responsibility of leading an entire people group into the land they'd longed after for over forty years!

Fortunately, Joshua had a lot going for him. Numbers 32:12 tells us that Joshua was fully devoted to God, Deuteronomy 34:9 explains that he was filled with wisdom, and First Kings 16:34 reveals that he was gifted as a prophet. Phillip Keller writes, "[Joshua] has seldom been given the full credit he deserves as perhaps the greatest man of faith ever to set foot on the stage of human history. His entire brilliant career was a straightforward story of simply setting down one foot after another in quiet compliance with the commands of his God."[12]

Joshua didn't try to be a hero, and he didn't seek recognition for himself. Instead, he trusted God's Word and waited on God's timing. His "secret" for staying close to God is revealed in Joshua 1:8: "This book of the law shall not depart from your mouth, but you shall meditate on it day and night, so that you may be careful to do according to all that is written in it; for then you will make your way prosperous, and then you will have success." In some ways, this verse is the key to the upgraded life.

There's little doubt that Joshua was God's man of the hour. God empowered him to possess his inheritance in the form of the Promised Land. Because of his faith, Joshua offers us a great example of living a victorious Christian life.

THE VICTORIOUS CHRISTIAN LIFE—WHAT IS IT?

Before we can discuss why Joshua's service was so exemplary, we have to look at the fundamentals of a faithful life. I've been talking a lot about "upgrading" your life, but I suppose that doesn't mean much if you don't first understand the basics.

As I mentioned before, the victorious Christian life is not some superior brand of Christianity that's reserved for super saints, missionaries and the elite elect. It is available for all who know Christ. In fact, it's *the life* Christ calls us to in the Gospels, and this message is reinforced in the Epistles.

Just because this life is available doesn't mean the upgrade is automatic. You don't randomly get struck with extra blessings. Instead, you have to commit to daily walking in faith. Look at the Israelites—they were told that Canaan was theirs, but they had to conquer the enemies living in the land in order to claim it.

Victorious living can occur even in our darkest hour. Salvation doesn't offer us freedom from trials—as evidenced by the struggles faced by godly men like Joshua and Paul. The abundant life is not a constant emotional high. It's lived in the midst of the evil, sin and conflicts of this world. As John Bisagno, former pastor of First Baptist Church in Houston, Texas, writes, "The Christian life was never intended to be a cessation of battle and spiritual warfare. Spiritual warfare is the raw material from which the fabric of success is woven for the Christian life."[13]

Because spiritual warfare is involved, there's no way a victorious life can be achieved through fleshly discipline and commitment. J. Oswald Sanders says it well: "Spiritual leadership . . . can never be generated by the self. There is no such thing as a self-made spiritual leader."[14] It's through *surrender* of our self-will that God grants victory. If you feel like you're failing in your Christian walk, it's probably because you're trying rather than trusting. God doesn't need your help, but He does expect your cooperation. You don't need to struggle toward victory; you need to stand firm in its promise. Don't go from failure to failure—remember that God is the one in control.

But that doesn't mean we should be passive. There's a difference between resting in His promises and rusting in our inactivity. The word "faith" comes from a Greek verb; it's meant to be active. Many Christians live in bondage to the old life, waiting for God to zap them into action. It doesn't work that way. Just as you don't become spiritual by trying to follow a lot of rules, you aren't spiritual when you allow yourself to grow comfortable in your surroundings and become stagnate. Waiting on God doesn't mean not doing anything—it means moving forward in faith and trusting Him for the victory!

FAITH FUELS VICTORY

During WWII my dad's brother was in the naval construction battalion called the Seabees. His crew would land on an island and construct roads and build camps there, preparing the area for the rest of the forces. I love the Seabees' slogan, which says, "The difficult we will do immediately; the impossible may take a little longer." The great thing about our God is the impossible doesn't take Him any longer. There is no difference in the eyes of God between the difficult and the "impossible."

God's Word promises victory—but that doesn't preclude troubles. God's work has to be done by God's people in God's power in God's way, but we still face battles. Without battles there aren't any heroes. Without struggles there aren't any conquerors. And without war there's no victory.

I mentioned before that Joshua is a good example of the victorious Christian life, but look at the things he had to go through! In Joshua 1:2 God told him, "Arise, cross this Jordan, you and all this people." At that time the Jordan was at flood stage and completely impassable. In other words, God told Joshua to take an impossible first step.

When God gives you a biblical directive, you have to trust it and act on it. You can seek biblical counsel, but don't allow anyone to talk you out of doing what God has called you to do—no matter how impossible it may seem. Take God at His Word.

Sometimes we have a hard time believing that God can operate outside of how things have always been done, but it's foolish to put God in a box. He has a way of pushing us outside our comfort zones to get us to the place He wants us to be. Faith might feel risky, but you can trust God to work out His purposes.

DESTROY VICTORY'S ENEMIES!

To walk in victory, you can't get trapped by worldly or fleshly desires along the way. If you're serious about wanting God to work in your life, you need to identify the enemies that will try to stagger your trust in the Lord and steal your blessings.

Joshua was told to lead the Israelites into Canaan. Archeologists have determined that the Hittites—one of the tribes of Canaan—were a great and powerful people, and Canaan had strong, fortified cities. The land was rugged, and the going was rough. The odds didn't look too good for the home team.

Just because you're walking by faith doesn't mean God will make everything easy for you. But you don't need to make sense of your situation. Why? Because God is with you. God empowers you to overcome situations you'd never be able to handle in your own strength.

Joshua and the Israelites wouldn't have been able to conquer Canaan on their own power, but they had God on their side, and that was all that mattered. God used His people to carry out His judgment on the Canaanites. (Before you decide God was being too harsh, remember that we're finite in our understanding, whereas God is infinite in all things. Jesus often quoted out of Deuteronomy and gave His stamp of approval on the Old Testament Scriptures. If He didn't have a problem with God's judgment, we shouldn't either.)

You may be wondering how defeating an entire people group can be a sign of God's goodness. How can victory be real and joyous if it comes at such a serious cost? Victory is always costly. (For us, Christ has already paid the cost.) The seven nations God sent Israel to destroy were given a long probation. They knew of Jehovah's power, but they denied it. When they refused to repent, they had to be removed to prevent the spread of their immorality and spiritual depravity.

The Israelites weren't sent to Canaan to murder, rape and plunder; they were sent to eradicate the rampant sinfulness that existed there. Francis Schaeffer notes, "Many of the Canaanite cities have been dug up and one can see they were perverse. Their worship was complete rebellion against God; their statues were pornographic."[15]

God hates sin and won't negotiate with it; victory involves destroying the things within you that are contrary to His will. Believers who think they can play with sin are sadly mistaken. The Enemy will do all he can to convince us to settle for a few inconsistencies. To deal with sin, we have to die to it. Only by rejecting everything that is an enemy of God can you have fellowship—and thereby victory—in Him!

RECEIVING BLESSINGS REQUIRES OBEDIENCE

Faith demands action. The only way to move from God's promise to possession is performance. In other words, we only gain the blessings we appropriate through active faith and obedience. Joshua's job description was clear—he had to motivate people who had lived in relative peace in the desert for forty years to pick up and cross a river.

God's commission never negates human responsibility. Joshua's duty came with a four-hundred-year-old promise (Deut. 6:23), but the fulfillment of that promise depended on his obedience. In order to enter the Promised Land, Joshua had to align his actions with the Lord's will. The Lord issued a serious charge to Joshua:

> Be strong and courageous, for you shall give this people possession of the land which I swore to their fathers to give them.

Only be strong and very courageous; be careful to do according to all the law which Moses My servant commanded you; do not turn from it to the right or to the left, so that you may have success wherever you go. This book of the law shall not depart from your mouth, but you shall meditate on it day and night, so that you may be careful to do according to all that is written in it; for then you will make your way prosperous, and then you will have success. Have I not commanded you? Be strong and courageous! Do not tremble or be dismayed, for the Lord your God is with you wherever you go. (1:6–9)

Do you see the repetition? God says, "do according to all *the law*," "the book of *the law* shall not depart from your mouth," and "be careful to do according to all that is written in [*the law*]." God emphasized one key element of obedience: devotion to the Word. The recorded Scriptures were to be Joshua's manual of instruction. In the books of Moses, Joshua would find his marching orders and the plan for his war campaign.

When God told Joshua to "meditate" on the book of the law, He used the Hebrew verb that means "to mutter." It was a Jewish practice to read Scripture out loud and then mull over it, allowing it to simmer in the soul. Joshua needed to *know* the Word in his heart as well as in his mind.

If you don't know the Word, you can't obey the Word. Colossians 3:16 instructs, "Let the word of Christ richly dwell within you." The psalmist also exulted, "Oh how I love Thy law! It is my meditation all the day" (119:97).

The secret to success is leading a life that honors God—and that comes from conforming to His Word. Alan Redpath once wrote, "I have no magic formula for your holiness; I have no hocus pocus treatment to offer you; I have no shortcut to spiritual power for any of you. All I can do is to say to you: Get back to your Bible, 'meditate on it day and night' and go down before God on your face in prayer."[16]

The order to follow God is simple: know His Word and pray to Him for the wisdom and strength to obey it. Then no matter what trials you face, He'll lead you through them!

NEVER FEAR!

Claiming victory in the Lord frees you from all fear. God is all-powerful. He has the ability to bring you through every situation He leads you into, and you can rely on His strength.

God promised the Israelites in Deuteronomy 12:10, "But you will cross the Jordan and settle in the land the LORD your God is giving you as an inheritance, and he will give you rest from all your enemies around you so that you will live in safety" (NIV). This same God cares for you and will be with you and will equip you to stand in victory.

The power God offers you is backed up by His promises.

(1) *Resurrection power.* Because Jesus died on the cross for you, conquered death and arose in all strength, you get to share in His victory! Ephesians 1:18–21 confirms this promise:

> I pray that the eyes of your heart may be enlightened, so that you will know what is the hope of His calling, what are the riches of the glory of His inheritance in the saints, and what is the surpassing greatness of His power toward us who believe. These are in accordance with the working of the strength of His might which He brought about in Christ, when He raised Him from the dead and seated Him at His right hand in the heavenly places, far above all rule and authority and power and dominion, and every name that is named, not only in this age but also in the one to come.

Christ is in charge and has your life under control, so you don't need to be afraid!

(2) *Reigning power.* After rising from the dead, Christ ascended to rule at His Father's right hand. He didn't just defeat

death for a set amount of time—He completely destroyed its power, and He's still reigning over it! Romans 5:17 tells us, "For if by the transgression of the one, death reigned through the one, much more those who receive the abundance of grace and of the gift of righteousness will reign in life through the One, Jesus Christ." You have freedom in Christ thanks to His grace and authority.

(3) *Released power.* Through the Holy Spirit you have all the power you need to do what God says. You can operate in His strength, with His mind-set and perspective, for "greater is He who is in you than he who is in the world" (1 John 4:4). Although Joshua was told to come against seven strong nations, he was instructed not to fear because his Lord was working through him. Paul drove this concept home in Colossians 1:29: "And for this purpose also I labor, striving according to His power, which mightily works within me." Accept Christ's might and His help!

GOD'S MARCHING ORDERS

Lehman Strauss was a great Bible teacher of the twentieth century. I got to know Lehman in his later years. His knowledge of the Word was beyond my ability to comprehend. One day I discovered why he took the Word of God so seriously. He showed me his Bible, and on the front was embossed in gold, "GOD'S WORD for Lehman Strauss." He told me, "God wants to speak to me through this Word. He has given me my marching orders. He tells me what paths to take. He leads me in righteousness. I just have to report for duty and read my orders for the day." How simple. How profound.

Living an upgraded life comes with a great responsibility. You have to enter into God's promises by studying and trusting His Word. Only then will you experience God's presence and partake in His vow, "I will never desert you, nor will I ever forsake you" (Heb. 13:5). Then you have to exercise the power that God has given you! The Lord of the universe desires to work in and through you; who are you to deny Him?

Now that you know what a victorious Christian life is and how to get it, you have no excuse to settle for an apathetic faith. Your epitaph doesn't have to read "What Could Have Been," "Died Defeated," or "Never Embraced All God Had for Him."

God didn't send His Son to save you just to keep you out of hell. His goal is for you to be formed into the image of Christ. Your transformation into all God has for you is at the very heart of Scripture. God can deal with any problem that comes your way. Lay aside your old, sinful habits and enter into your inheritance in Christ.

Victory involves walking by the faith that Jesus has already won and that has empowered you to possess God's promises. As Ron Dunn once said, "Victory is not doing your best for Jesus; it is Jesus doing His best for you." God isn't calling you to individual victory; He's calling you to the Victor—to the One who is your victory.

Want an upgraded Christian life? Trust in Christ's victory and all the power, blessing and glory it holds!

Do Something!
Claim Your Upgrade

LIVING in southwest Georgia, it rarely gets cold enough for a fire (unless we also turn on the air conditioner). But when we are in the mountains, we love having a fire going. I enjoy settling down with my family in front of a fire, listening to the logs crackle and watching the light from the flames dance around the room.

Having daughters, it has become my job to maintain warmth in the house. I buy the fire starter and kindling wood, and I make sure the log rack by the fireplace is well-stocked. Quite a bit of work goes into building a fire; it isn't all about relaxation. And keeping a fire burning takes effort! I have to tend to it—prodding the logs to get air to the embers. If I don't pay attention and add fuel, the fire will die.

Just like fires, it's possible for us to lose our spark. Before we know it, the fire that once burned brightly dies down. Unless we look after the fires in our hearts, constantly building them up, they can burn out.

We need to continually stir up our hearts to be on fire for the Lord. The upgraded life comes with a great responsibility. Even though God is the One who ultimately has to do the work in our lives, our role is not passive. If we want to see a work of God, we need to seek it!

THE DESIRE FOR GOD TO STIR HIMSELF

Having an upgraded life starts with humbling ourselves before the Lord and seeking His face. We need to come before God and cry out to Him to kindle afresh His Spirit in our lives. The psalmist frequently asked for the Lord to renew His presence in his life. In Psalm 35:23 he cried, "*Stir up Yourself*," and in 80:1–2 he said, "Oh, give ear, Shepherd of Israel, You who lead Joseph like a flock . . . *stir up Your power* and come to save us!"

Psalm 80 is filled with David asking God to heed his prayers. In verses 1–3 David urged God to hear; in 4–7 he petitioned God to heal; and in 8–19 he pleaded to God for help. David knew he couldn't save himself, so he turned to the One who could create a new work in his heart.

In the New Testament Christ is referred to as the Good Shepherd. He's our Shepherd, and we're His sheep. Have you ever seen sheep that are left to wander? They are by nature wayward, dumb animals that are unable to intelligently process their surroundings. They can't survive in the wild; they need guidance. There's no such thing as a self-shepherded sheep. Like sheep, we're lost without Christ's direction. This is why we need to seek the Lord's leading.

God doesn't drive unwilling followers; He leads those who desire to follow after Him. As the leader, He sees the opportunities and difficulties we're going to face long before we do. But He can't show us the way if we won't follow. We have to seek revival and turn our faces toward Him, watching where He leads us.

Psalm 80 is a prayer of revival. The psalmist called for God, the Shepherd of Israel, to lead and refresh His people. Three times in this passage—in verses 3, 7 and 19—David cried out, "Restore us!" Recognizing the backsliding that had occurred, the psalmist prayed for the Shepherd to turn His face toward His people in their time of distress.

No matter what you're going through, it's always a good move to turn to the Lord and pray for Him to move afresh in your life. When God stirs in your life, you know it. If you want Him to stir, you have to seek Him, then obey His Word and allow His Spirit to work in you and through you.

THE DEMAND TO STIR OURSELVES

In addition to asking the Lord to move, we need to stir ourselves. Christianity doesn't operate in a vacuum; heaven's enablement is coupled with human responsibility. Second Timothy 1:6–7 says, "For this reason I remind you to kindle afresh the gift of God which is in you through the laying on of my hands. For God has not given us a spirit of timidity, but of power and love and discipline." "To kindle afresh" means to stir up. Paul didn't suggest Timothy try to reexperience some spiritual high from the past or to manufacture some feeling within himself. Instead he prayed that Timothy would experience the fullness of his gifting.

Timothy was in danger of falling into a rut. He wasn't making the spiritual progress Paul thought he should be. Paul was looking to pass the torch to the young preacher, and he wanted to make sure Timothy understood the importance of his calling. Paul wrote his second letter to Timothy to spur him on.

Don't think that Timothy needed a letter because he wasn't living correctly. Timothy was actually an upstanding young man, full of faith and godly heritage. He was a godly man and a good pastor—but he needed to keep the fire burning in his heart.

There's a very popular conference called Passion that's held every year in Atlanta around the first of the year. Many young people leave there impassioned for missions, with a heart to end slavery or sex trafficking. The way to maintain that desire to care for and act on things that matter to God is to passionately seek more of Him.

Do we have a passion for God? Does our passion carry over into our daily living? As I look at the Christian church, I don't see a strong passion for God, the lost, missions or evangelism. My hope is for the Millennial Generation to experience another Jesus movement like I experienced in the 1970s. They have seen the emptiness of their parents' pursuit of materialistic things. They long for purpose. My heart's desire is that a multitude of young men and women will be stirred to action for the cause of Christ.

The church today isn't lacking gifted preachers or impressive technology. Rather, it lacks people of God who are stirred up and eager to fulfill His purposes. You can be well-trained, seminary-educated and articulate about the Scriptures but still lack the empowerment of the Holy Spirit. A legalist, professor, pastor or leader of a Bible study can "know" the truth but not walk in the Spirit.

The Lord wouldn't issue the command for us to be stirred if we were already experiencing a fresh move of His Spirit. God never wastes words. He doesn't bother telling men who are awake to wake up or men who are lying down to lie down. We *need* a reawakening!

I can't tell you how many people I've met on my travels who have let life grind them down and church politics cool them off. Paul called Timothy to uncompromising commitment. In verses 8, 12 and 16, he stressed the importance of trusting God and being unashamed to proclaim His truths. Appealing to Timothy to step up for the sake of the gospel, Paul urged him to test his belief and trust his God.

Lest you decide Paul's message to Timothy is only for the Christian elite, let me give you a few facts to show that even though God had given Timothy a serious mission, he was just a normal guy.

1. Timothy was relatively young. Paul urged him in First Timothy 4:12, "Let no one look down on your youthfulness, but rather in speech, conduct, love, faith and purity, show yourself an example of those who believe."

2. He had health issues. Paul mentioned Timothy's "frequent ailments" in First Timothy 5:23.

3. He was timid and introverted. Because he had such a strong mentor in Paul, Timothy was inclined to lean on others' guidance instead of to lead. Paul had to exhort him to stand his ground.

4. He didn't have it easy. Despite his calling, Timothy faced serious challenges. In Ephesus he had to confront heresy and organize several ministries. Timothy was leading at a time when the church was under increasing persecution. Threatened by apostasy, heresy and Gnosticism, the church's foundations were being shaken. Bishop Moule described this period dimly: "Christianity . . . trembled, humanly speaking, on the verge of annihilation."

You've probably heard it said that God doesn't call the equipped; He equips the called. This is quite true. And after you've accepted your calling, you need to be continually refreshed in the Spirit.

If you want to serve God, it doesn't matter what you look like, where you went to school, how good your résumé looks or how talented you are. Your abilities and enthusiasm are never going to make the mark. I heard Adrian Rogers say years ago,

"Some of us are too big for God to use." God often uses those we wouldn't naturally choose so that when His plans succeed, no one can take the glory that only He deserves. You might feel like a weak Timothy, but God can use you.

Plain and simple—you have to rely on the Holy Spirit. Without the Spirit, there's no empowered prayer, true passion for the lost or unselfish love for the Creator.

But just because the Spirit is acting on your behalf doesn't mean you'll have it easy. Christians experience times when the fires of God burn low. Several things can douse your fire, including the desire to be successful, famous, revered in others' eyes, like those "in the world." Life will wear you down. You're fighting a spiritual battle.

We often bail out on God, rejecting His calling for our own selfish wants. For Timothy, identifying himself with Christ meant facing persecution, and identifying himself with Paul meant facing possible imprisonment. Standing on the Scriptures meant coming under fire from the Judaizers and Gnostics. But God didn't call Timothy to hide; He called him to action!

In verse 2:3 of his second letter to Timothy, Paul exhorted, "Suffer hardship with me, as a good soldier of Christ Jesus." When life gets tough, it's no time to go AWOL. When others sound the retreat, God is calling you to sound the charge!

Look at the charge Timothy was given. In 1:14 he's told to guard the gospel. In 2:3, 8 and 9, he's told to suffer for the gospel. In 3:13–14 he's told to continue in the gospel, and in 4:1–2 he's told to proclaim the gospel. See a common thread? Timothy's entire calling was wrapped up in boldly sharing the good news—regardless of the consequences. Paul wanted Timothy on the front lines, not behind the lines in the battle.

While the church in America isn't under open physical persecution like in Ephesus, it's facing subtle but serious attacks from the Enemy. Messages are being watered down to please crowds, and the health and wealth prosperity gospel is rampant. False teachers write bestselling "Christian" books. Pastors are gray on areas that are clearly black-and-white in God's Word. Add to that the constant undermining of the Christian worldview in our judicial system, and it's past time for us to stir ourselves up. When we're on fire for God, it shows. And when we aren't on fire—that shows too.

A couple of years ago I sat in on a youth conference that made me want to scream. Teens shuffled into the convention center with their heads down, their shoulders slumped and their faces downcast. The majority of them were texting rather than talking to those around them. Watching these kids, all I could think was *They don't look like they have anything a lost person would want or need*. I'm not just trying to come down hard on young people. I've seen adults who think the purpose of coming to church is to sit, soak and sour.

Sadly, many Christians—even pastors, staff members, deacons, elders, those who sing in the choir and lead ministries—walk around looking depressed and downtrodden. We've done something the enemies of the church couldn't do: we've made following Christ boring. Surely Jesus died for more than this! In Matthew 24:12 Jesus said, "Because lawlessness is increased, most people's love will grow cold." We can't afford to have cold love, because the world is desperately in need of a burning passion for God.

So how do we keep the fire alive? Paul urged Timothy not to grow weary—allowing the pressures of the day to turn him into an ordinary preacher. It's likely that Timothy had become fearful of opposition or had grown weary in his pastoral work. Paul challenged Timothy to act on the promises of God. The Lord has given us these same promises.

We're called to consistency. Every day we need to wake up, put on the armor of God and walk in the fullness of the Spirit. Don't look for a feeling when you need a filling. We need a rekindling and then a daily kindling afresh of holy fire.

A revived church is a unified body of revived individuals. You can't just sit back and wait for the pastor or someone else to strike flame into your heart. Note that Paul didn't say to Timothy, "Let me rekindle a flame in you." No, he said, "*You* rekindle your flame." Like Timothy, you have to make loving the Lord and following His commands your highest priority. If your fire is burning out, it's up to you to stir yourself and seek the Spirit.

THE DECISION TO STIR YOURSELF

One time all the fires went out in a small village in Scotland. The people couldn't cook, and it was winter, so they were cold. Matches hadn't been invented yet, so a band of men set out to find fire. After much searching, they found one cottage that was glowing. The owners of the cottage welcomed them in, and the men lit torches and carried the fire back to their homes.

Like those village dwellers, there are people in this world who are discouraged, weary and cold. They are searching for fire. They need Christians who have stirred their hearts for God and who are burning for Him. If they came to your house, would they see a saint on fire? If they walked into your church on a typical Sunday, would they find a body of believers on fire for God? If not, why?

Revival might have to start the fire with a handful of kindling wood, and it may take a while to dry out the wet logs of dead faith lying around the church. But once lit, God's light shines brightly.

Unfortunately, many churchgoers allow their fire for God to die out. All it takes to kill a fire is neglect. Similarly, all it takes for your faith to grow cold is for you to get lazy and ignore your time with God. We can be like Jesus's disciples—falling asleep in the garden when God wants us to pray and seek His will.

Wake up! It's easy to get accustomed to going to church and knowing the truth and to take these things for granted. At the church I pastor, we call it "checking the boxes." We have offering envelopes on which you can check that you're giving, attending Bible study, praying, etc. You can check the box without having a warm heart for God. Just because you have a fireplace doesn't mean you have a fire going.

We're called to stand against the current of this world. Re-kindling God's flame often involves going against the grain to proclaim the message of the gospel—no matter how radical and unconventional a message of sacrifice and service might seem in this self-centered culture. Choose now to be of a sincere mind.

Those at the pulpits and in the pews need to be filled with a sense of urgency. The Enemy will always take full advantage of a lethargic believer or church. We can't afford to settle. If the altar isn't full at every service with people whose lives are being saved and transformed, we need to fall before God. We need to stir ourselves. We can't just talk about how we want a fresh work of the Spirit in our lives while allowing ourselves to continue down the same path—we have to act and truly *seek* the Lord.

So what does that look like? Two of the main ways to tend to God's fire are to (1) read your Bible and (2) maintain your prayer relationship with the Lord. You've heard the importance of these two actions stressed time and again, but are you doing them? Knowing the right thing to do is useless if you don't act!

When you read the Scriptures, you find several important calls to action. First Thessalonians 5:1–11 tells us to wake up; First John 2:28–3:3 tells us to clean up; Romans 13:14 tells us to grow up; and Second Timothy 1:6 tells us to stir ourselves up.

All these things are essential for a full, upgraded Christian life.

If the devil can't keep you from being saved, he'll work to make you average. God hasn't given us a spirit of fear (2 Tim. 1:7), so you can be assured that whatever you're afraid of—whatever is holding you back from fully serving the Lord—is not of God. "Do this, knowing the time, that it is already the hour for you to awaken from sleep; for now salvation is nearer to us than when we believed. The night is almost gone, and the day is near. Therefore let us lay aside the deeds of darkness and put on the armor of light" (Rom. 13:11–12).

The upgraded life requires obedience and an active effort to stir yourself to keep your love for God burning. I'm reminded of the childhood hymn that says, "This little light of mine, I'm gonna let it shine. Let it shine, let it shine, let it shine."

You're responsible for tending the fire of the Holy Spirit that God has placed in your heart. If the church doesn't shine her light, how will this dark world see God's brilliant glory?

GET HELP! ACCEPT THE SPIRIT'S EMPOWERMENT

ABOUT every three years I have to purchase a new computer. Due to either general wear and tear, an outdated operating system or a lack of storage space, I'm forced to upgrade in order to be effective and efficient.

Let's say I bought the best possible computer with the fastest operating system and the largest hard drive available. I would bring it home, pull it out of the box and start hooking it up. But what if I forgot to plug it in? I could call the store, complain and demand my money back—but at the end of the day, I would be at fault for not availing myself of the power.

Do you see the connection? Like computers, we weren't created to function on our own. We need to be connected. Unless we're plugged into God's power, we'll never become the people He has called us to be. To operate in our flesh is to operate disconnected from the power of God.

In chapter four I discussed how offending the Holy Spirit will disqualify you for an upgrade. That's because the Spirit is our mediator. He intercedes to the Father on our behalf and guides us in our Christian walk. It's impossible to lead a victorious Christian life without His enablement. Without the Spirit, you will stumble, fall and fail. It is in His power that we stand and succeed. You need to be plugged into the Spirit; you need to know who He is and to understand His role in your upgraded life.

WHO IS THE SPIRIT?

Before learning about the Spirit's role in your life, it's important to understand His historical significance. Some mistakenly believe that the Holy Spirit didn't exist until Pentecost (Acts 2). But He is an eternal part of the Godhead. The Holy Spirit was present at creation. (Genesis 1:2 says, "The Spirit of God was moving over the surface of the waters," and Genesis 1:26 uses the first person plural pronoun—"Let *us* make man.") Those who worked on the Tabernacle were empowered by the Spirit (Exod. 31:3). The Spirit of God came upon Gideon (Judg. 6:34).

We know from the nativity story that the Spirit was responsible for the virgin birth (Matt. 1:20) and present at the Incarnation. He was there at the beginning of the church. In the New Testament Jesus said the Spirit would abide with us forever (John 14:16). Second Timothy 3:16 tells us that "all Scripture is inspired by God," and Second Peter 1:21 says, "No prophecy was ever made by an act of human will, but men moved by the Holy Spirit spoke from God."

Despite His presence in Scripture, I'd venture to say that the role of the Holy Spirit is one of the most misunderstood doctrines. We are prone to argue about the Spirit based on our denomination, doctrinal preferences or experiences, but the standard for studying and applying the Spirit's work to our lives is the inerrant Word of God.

The Spirit longs to do great things in and through us. Don't hinder His work by failing to recognize His presence! At the time of the transition from the Old Testament to the Christian church, Paul came across some believers in Ephesus who were unaware of the Spirit. When he asked some disciples if they had received the Holy Spirit when they believed, they replied, "No, we have not even heard that there is a Holy Spirit" (Acts 19:2). Don't be part of the ignorant brethren referenced in the Epistles (Rom. 1:13, 11:25; 1 Cor. 10:1, 12:1; 2 Cor. 1:8; 1 Thess. 4:13).

While 99 percent of you who are reading this book know about the Spirit, the question remains: are you operating in His power? Are you plugged in?

Let's start with the basics. In college you normally can't take a 201 or a 301 course until you've passed the 101 class. Before we can study the deep things of God, we have to learn the fundamentals.

The Holy Spirit is a person. When Jesus talked about the Spirit in John 14:16–17, He referred to Him using the pronouns "He" and "Him." The Holy Spirit is not an "it." The Spirit has emotions, an intellect and a will. He is not a force or an energy field; He is a being. He can be grieved (Eph. 4:30), He can be exasperated (Isa. 63:10), He can love (Rom. 15:30), He can think (1 Cor. 2:10), and He can choose to act (First Corinthians 12:11 says He distributes gifts "as He wills"). The Spirit is a person, not a puppet to move at our every whim. Rather, we need to open ourselves to be used by Him.

The Holy Spirit is divine. The Holy Spirit is God Himself. The Trinity consists of God the Father, God the Son and God the Spirit. Each member plays a unique and important role. The Father plans, the Son implements and the Spirit consummates. In John 14:16 Jesus said He would ask the Father to send "another Helper." Jesus didn't promise a second-rate substitute; the word used for "another" is a word meaning another of the same kind, just like the first! The Holy Spirit wasn't sent to replace God. God was with His people in the Tabernacle, Jesus was with His disciples in the physical body, and now the Spirit is in us, allowing us access to the Father and counseling us in our daily walks. A.T. Pierson writes,

> The Spirit of God, the Paraclete, is to be to the disciples and to the church all that Christ would have been had He tarried among us and been the personal companion and counselor of each and all. And by the Spirit of God working in and through the believer and the church, believers are, in their measure, to be to the world what the Spirit is to them.[17]

The Holy Spirit is holy. This one might sound a little redundant, but it's imperative to remember that the word "holy" defines the Spirit's character. "Holy" means to be undefiled and set apart for a special purpose. The role of the Holy Spirit is to set us apart from sin—which sets us apart for God (John 16:8–11). On our own we could never meet God's standards of cleanliness.

I'll admit that I'm a neat freak. I don't just like things to *appear* clean; I need them to *be* clean. But even if I scrubbed for my entire lifetime, I'd never be able to make myself clean like the Holy Spirit can. Tony Evans points out, "We are so unlike God, we don't know how holy holy is." The Spirit scours our bodies, souls and spirits so that we can be temples of the Lord.

The Holy Spirit lives in believers. One of the reasons the Spirit wants to keep the temple clean is because He lives in it; He lives in us. How can the Holy Spirit function in an unholy vessel?

The Spirit performs several essential functions in and through us. Numerous authors have pointed out the following traits (and many others in addition to these), but they are worth repeating.

- He speaks. Scripture repeatedly references the Spirit's talking: "the Spirit said" (Acts 13:2), "the Spirit says" (1 Tim. 4:1), and "hear what the Spirit says to the churches" (Rev. 2:7).
- He intercedes to the Father. Romans 8:26 tells us, "The Spirit Himself intercedes for us with groanings too deep for words."
- He witnesses to us. Jesus said, "He [the Holy Spirit] will testify about Me" (John 15:26).
- He teaches us. Jesus said, "He [the Holy Spirit] will teach you all things" (John 14:26).
- He fellowships with us. The Spirit is our constant companion. Paul ended his second letter to the Corinthians with "the grace of the Lord Jesus Christ, and the love of God, and *the fellowship of the Holy Spirit*, be with you all."
- He guides us. We should seek to follow the Spirit's leading. In Acts 16:6–7 the Spirit kept His servants from going to certain areas.
- He does the supernatural. In Romans 15:19 Paul wrote, "In the power of signs and wonders, *in the power of the Spirit* . . . I have fully preached the gospel of Christ."

The Holy Spirit is a central member of the Trinity and our Comforter and Strengthener who leads us in all truth and righteousness. He has not left us as helpless orphans. Because of this, He deserves our obedience.

When the movie *Ben-Hur* was being filmed, actor Charlton Heston had to learn to drive a chariot. He went to the director and said, "I can barely stay on this thing. How am I supposed to win the race in this scene?" The director told him, "Your job is just to stay on the chariot. It's my job to make sure you win."

Our job is to stay in the race. We must obey the command to be filled. We are not commanded to be sealed with or baptized in the Spirit, but we are commanded to be *filled* with the Spirit. Remember that unless you're filled with the Spirit, you will lack supernatural power and your life won't reveal the miraculous.

THE FILLING OF THE SPIRIT

I remember preaching in an outdoor tabernacle at Falls Creek in Oklahoma in the summer of 1995. The temperature was 105 degrees, and under the stage lights on the platform, it was around 120. By the time I finished preaching, I was drenched in sweat and feeling dehydrated.

When I got out of that tabernacle, I immediately started drinking bottles of water, one right after the other. I couldn't get enough water in my system. I was physically drained and dry.

There are times when I've felt this dry spiritually. Even as a pastor, I've gone through periods when my life looked like a dried-up well or a water line clogged with too much busyness to get alone with the Lord. At those times the refreshing water of the Word was not flowing through me.

If you take a careful look at the average Christian or church, you'll see little evidence of the fullness of the Spirit. Our services lack conviction, power, brokenness, true worship and a deep longing for God. We go through the motions and oil the machinery, but there is no power. Our spiritual tanks are empty, and we're running on fumes while singing songs declaring our tanks are full. Yet in the back of our minds, we're really wondering if we have enough of God to get us through the next week.

Too often believers find themselves living Jeremiah 2:13: "For My people have committed two evils: they have forsaken Me, the fountain of living waters, to hew for themselves cisterns, broken cisterns that can hold no water." When believers experience this dryness, they often fall away from God—seeking any kind of "spiritual feeling" possible. But no earthly fountain can satisfy. Fame, fortune, power and pleasure all run dry. Rather than running to God and finding their way to an altar, they let their dry existence take them out the back door, looking to the world for a substitute.

Thankfully, Scripture teaches us a way to be fully satiated. In John 7:37–39 Jesus explained that the Spirit is living water that flows through us. "On the last day, the great day of the feast, Jesus stood and cried out, saying, 'If anyone is thirsty, let him come to Me and drink. He who believes in Me, as the Scripture said, "From his innermost being will flow rivers of living water."' But this He spoke of the Spirit, whom those who believed in Him were to receive; for the Spirit was not yet given because Jesus was not yet glorified."

Note that Christ doesn't limit the Spirit's power as only for a redeemed elite. His promise was made to people who had religion but no power. They celebrated the great Feast of Tabernacles, but they had fallen into religious ruts and forgotten the Lord. They didn't even recognize the living God when He stood before them. Yet *anyone* who believes in Christ has access to the living water of the Spirit. The Spirit offers *every believer* continuous, abundant refreshment and fulfillment. He is an artesian well of flowing, refreshing power.

The Holy Spirit is the supernatural, sustaining life force of the believer. We need Him much like a fish needs water to survive and thrive. Warren Wiersbe explains, "Water for drinking is one of the symbols of the Holy Spirit in the Bible. Water for washing is a symbol of the Word of God (John 15:3; Eph. 5:26). Just as water satisfies thirst and produces fruitfulness, so the Spirit of God satisfies the inner person and enables us to bear fruit."

Some Christians seem to want the fruit without the root. Let me explain. If we want to display the fruit of God's working in our lives (power, victory), then we can't ignore the nourishing, stabilizing root of the Holy Spirit. Charles Spurgeon urged, "Let us not be satisfied with the sip that saves, but let us go on to that which buries the flesh and raises us in the likeness of the risen Lord—even into the Holy Spirit, and into fire which makes us spiritual and sets us all on flame with zeal for the glory of God, and eagerness for usefulness by which that glory may be increased among the sons of men."

WHY DO WE NEED THE SPIRIT?

The Spirit can't fully operate in your life until you give Him complete control. Your life is like a glove. Gloves don't move on their own. Without a hand in them, they don't serve their protective purpose. Similarly, unless the Holy Spirit fills up every part of your life, you'll never be able to function according to your created purpose. You'll live spiritually dehydrated when God has so much more for you.

What makes me so sure the Spirit is essential to your faith? To answer that question we have to go back to the time before Christ's crucifixion. When Jesus told His disciples He was going to be betrayed and killed, they got nervous. Then He said something that made no sense to them: "I'm about to go; you guys carry on until I return." They wondered, *How can we go without Jesus?!* They had to be thinking of how they had given up their jobs and risked their lives to follow Him. They had to be asking: How will we make it if You leave? How are we supposed to keep from being upset about this? *Please say You're kidding.*

The answer to their questions is our answer as well. When Christ was preparing to leave this earth, He made a promise to His disciples. He said,

> I will ask the Father, and He will give you another Helper, that He may be with you forever; that is the Spirit of truth, whom the world cannot receive, because it does not see Him or know

Him, but you know Him because He abides with you and will be in you. I will not leave you as orphans; I will come to you. (John 14:16–18)

Jesus sent the Holy Spirit to be with His disciples so they might remember all He had taught and could continue growing in their faith (14:26). As Christ's followers, we are filled with that same Spirit, and He guides and grows us.

The Holy Spirit does *in* us what Jesus did *for* us. Being a strong Christian isn't about feeling a certain way or even knowing specific things but about *receiving* the supernatural results the Spirit will work in you. David Jeremiah once noted that almost every central doctrine is rooted in the gifts and ministry of the Holy Spirit. Without the Holy Spirit, our faith is powerless and we are helpless.

Therefore, it's important to know exactly who the Spirit is. Again, what I'm about to share has been covered by many authors and books, but it bears repeating because it is so essential. Scripture gives us several specific tasks and responsibilities of the Holy Spirit.

He is the agent of salvation. Salvation is a supernatural work of God. The flesh has no power to save. Good works do not save. Baptism does not save. Joining a church does not save. You can't be saved by leaning on someone else's faith. Salvation only comes through being convicted by the Holy Spirit. God begins to press in on us, and we see we are lost and in need of a Savior. God applies His Word to the human heart through His Holy Spirit who convicts us and leads us to repent.

The Gospel of John tells us, "Unless one is born of water and the Spirit, he cannot enter into the kingdom of God" (3:3, 5). The Holy Spirit makes men new in Christ: "He saved us, not on the basis of deeds which we have done in righteousness, but according to His mercy, by the washing of regeneration and renewing by the Holy Spirit" (Titus 3:5). When we are alive in the Spirit, He assures us of our relationship with God: "The Spirit Himself bears witness with our spirit that we are children of God" (Rom. 8:16).

He is the agent of sanctification. Second Thessalonians 2:13 tells us, "God has chosen you from the beginning for salvation through sanctification by the Spirit and faith in the truth." The same Spirit who saves is the Spirit who works in our sanctification. Christ's salvation sets us apart from the world, and the Holy Spirit continues this work of growing us to be more and more like Christ. Ron Dunn said, "The Spirit of God works in sanctification to make us more like Jesus so that when we get to heaven, we won't be so shocked."

In sanctification the Spirit works in us and through us. First Corinthians explicitly states, "Your body is the temple of the Holy Spirit who is in you, whom you have from God" (6:19). This indwelling of the Spirit plugs us into the power we do not have on our own. Left to ourselves, we could not be saved or renewed.

He allows us access to God's throne. The Spirit marks Christians as belonging to the Father. "In Him, you also, after listening to the message of truth, the gospel of your salvation—having also believed, you were sealed in Him with the Holy Spirit of promise, who is given as a pledge of our inheritance" (Eph. 1:13–14). We as believers are sealed for God's kingdom through the Spirit. Ephesians 6:18 challenges us to "pray at all times in the Spirit." In addition to confirming our salvation and leading us in holiness, the Spirit interprets our prayers to the Lord. Romans 8:26 says, "We do not know how to pray as we should, but the Spirit Himself intercedes for us with groanings too deep for words." The Spirit translates what we're trying to convey to our Holy God.

He is the administrator of spiritual gifts. First Corinthians 12:4–11 explains that the Spirit grants us gifts that allow us to serve others in the body of Christ. Each gift is important to the church's functioning, and when combined, they allow believers to experience the fullness of the Spirit. (The danger I sometimes see when people talk about the Holy Spirit is that they get caught up in the gifts more than the Giver. When that happens, we downgrade our lives. God is the Giver, and He decides what we need. We shouldn't beg for gifts. We should long for the Holy Spirit to guide us.)

He empowers our witnessing. In Acts 1:8 Christ explained, "You will receive power when the Holy Spirit has come upon you; and you shall be My witnesses . . . even to the remotest part of the earth." It's only through the Spirit's empowerment that we're able to fulfill the Great Commission.

Remember, the Peter at Pentecost was the same Peter who only a few weeks before had denied Christ. Something happened. Something supernatural took place in Peter. He was a different man. He was bold, not in his flesh as he had been in the past, but in the Spirit.

He enables our obedience. First Peter 1:23 and James 1:18 confirm that the Spirit works in accordance with the Word of God. The Word reveals God's promises to us, and the Spirit makes them a reality. You need the Spirit to activate the Scriptures in your heart. To say that you can't obey what God has requested is to deny the work of regeneration being done by the Spirit.

He transforms us into His image. The Holy Spirit invades our being and *transforms* our spirit. Second Corinthians 3:18 says, "But we all, with unveiled face, beholding as in a mirror the glory of the Lord, are being transformed into the same image from glory to glory, just as from the Lord, the Spirit." This way when the Father looks at us, He sees the beauty of His Spirit reflected instead of our own sinful nature. As Vance Havner said, "The Lord didn't come to give us a tune-up but an overhaul. The work of the Spirit is not an old Adam improvement society."

He reveals God's wisdom to us. The Spirit illuminates and reveals the things of the Lord to us. "For to us God revealed them [things not seen, the things God has prepared] through the Spirit; for the Spirit searches all things, even the depths of God . . . The thoughts of God no one knows except the Spirit of God" (1 Cor. 2:10–11).

He illuminates the Scriptures. You can't understand the Bible without knowing the Author. The Holy Spirit opens our minds to understand God's Word.

> Now we have received, not the spirit of the world, but the Spirit who is from God, that we might know the things freely given to us by God which things we also speak, not in words taught by human wisdom, but in those taught by the Spirit, combining spiritual thoughts with spiritual words. But a natural man does not accept the things of the Spirit of God; for they are foolishness to him, and he cannot understand them, because they are spiritually appraised. (1 Cor. 2:12–14)

Spiritual truths require the *Spirit*ual interpreter.

He sets us apart to do God's work. The New Testament tells us that we are anointed by the Spirit of God. Verses 20 and 27 of First John 2 tell us, "You have an anointing from the Holy One . . . The anointing which you received from Him abides in you, and you have no need for anyone to teach you; but His anointing teaches you all things, and is true and is not a lie, and just as it has taught you, you abide in Him."

The word "anointing" is reminiscent of the Old Testament practice of pouring oil on the heads of those set apart for a special purpose. Every Christ-follower has this anointing. Warren Wiersbe writes, "It is not necessary for you to pray for 'an anointing of the Spirit'; if you are a Christian, you have already received this special anointing. This anointing 'abides in us' and therefore does not need to be imparted to us."[18]

"Abide" means to remain in fellowship; therefore First John tells us to remain relationally close to Christ. When we do so, His Spirit will teach us, and we will bear fruit, more fruit, much fruit and fruit that remains. First John reminds us that when listening to teachings, we must ask the Spirit to guide us into all truth. Then, with the enablement of the Spirit, we must act on that truth to do God's will.

BE SPIRIT-FILLED

When we came into the world, our minds were blind to truth. We are, by nature, fallen creatures. We have an old Adamic nature that is bent toward sin. We were born loving things we should hate and hating things we should love. Left to ourselves, we would live our entire lives fulfilling the works of the flesh, and the mind of the flesh is hostile toward God (Rom. 8:7).

The good news is that when we're saved, the Holy Spirit imparts to us a new nature, a new mind. R.A. Torrey explained, "No amount of preaching, no matter how orthodox it may be, no amount of mere study of the Word will regenerate unless the Holy Spirit works. It is He and He alone who makes a man a new creature."

Time and time again Scripture references the importance of walking a Spirit-filled life. Look at these verses pulled from Acts: "Peter, *filled with the Holy Spirit . . .*" (4:8); "When [Peter, John and their people] had prayed, the place where they had gathered together was shaken, and they were all *filled with the Holy Spirit*, and began to speak the Word of God with boldness" (4:31); "Select from among you seven men of good reputation, *full of the Spirit* and of wisdom . . ." (6:3); Christ sent Ananias to Paul so that he might "see again and *be filled with the Holy Spirit*" (9:17); Barnabas was described as being "a good man, and *full of the Holy Spirit* and of faith" (11:24); Paul was said to be "*filled with the Holy Spirit*" (13:9); "And the disciples were continually *filled* with joy and *with the Holy Spirit*" (13:52). Do you see the emphasis on living in the Spirit's fullness?

The church will have success in direct proportion to its walking in the fullness of God's Spirit. We are rarely shaken by a move of the Spirit, so we lack the boldness to confront our world. We lack joy because we lack the continual renewal that comes when the Spirit dwells within us. So let's break this down to the basics. How can believers be filled with the Spirit and satisfied?

We have to thirst. In 2010 my youngest daughter Hayley went to Uganda to help install a fresh water well. Before they had a well, the people were drinking out of the same stagnant pools as the cattle. The water was polluted, infested and unfit to drink. A new well changed everything.

Westerners don't value the water we get from our tap in the same way those in third-world countries value the water they've traveled miles to get from a well. Most of us have never experienced being without water, so we don't know what it's like to desperately seek it. But rather than nonchalantly "sampling" the Spirit, we need to crave His presence in our lives. Until we admit we're parched, we can't have our thirst quenched.

We have to come. We're willing to ask God to forgive our sins and take them away, but then we don't forsake them. We keep returning to the same things. We go back to the same broken cisterns. Until we have a clean break, we will never live the life God intended. It requires turning from sin and coming to Him in full surrender. Coming to God means falling at His feet and abandoning all our concepts of self-worth to Him. Only when we come to Him with everything and for everything can His rivers of living water flow through us.

Once we believe, we have to receive. A thirsty man has to drink to quench his thirst; John 7:39 says, "those who believed in [the Spirit] were to receive." Believing and receiving is: (1) the law of salvation (John 1:12 says, "But as many as received Him, to them He gave the power to become the sons of God; even to those that believe on His name."), (2) the law of prayer (Mark 11:24 says, "All things for which you pray and ask, believe that you have received them, and they shall be granted you.") and (3) the law of the Spirit.

We are filled when we take God at His Word by faith. Don't worry about *feeling* something. Believe, receive the filling of the Spirit and then believe that you have received!

We should overflow. When living water flows in and through us, we will give evidence of His power. The church has never had so many programs and resources and so little life. We need to believe in who the Spirit is and what He's doing. We need to thirst after Him, come before Him, drink deeply of Him, believe in Him and overflow with His power. As the hymnist George Atkins wrote, "Brethren we have met to worship and adore the Lord our God. Will you pray with all your power, while we try to preach the Word? All is vain unless the Spirit of the Holy One comes down. Brethren pray and Holy Manna will be showered all around."

In closing, I urge you to follow the wise advice of Oswald Chambers: "Mind the Holy Spirit, mind His light, mind His convictions, mind His guidance, and slowly and surely the sensual personality will be turned into a spiritual personality."

Enjoying the Upgraded Life

KNOWING THE SHEPHERD

IMAGINE a dark night on a farm, sheep bleating weakly out in their pasture. There is a light wind, but otherwise the evening is quite still. Then a strange noise begins. Rough-looking men dressed in all black pile out of a van and start calling the sheep, trying to entice them to leave with them. The situation is ominous, but the sheep don't seem to be paying any attention. They continue happily grazing and wandering around with no sense of peril. You wonder *What's keeping the men from hopping the fence and taking the sheep? Why do the sheep seem so safe?*

If you're familiar with the gospels, you probably recognize this allegory. In John 10:7–11 Jesus said,

> Truly, truly, I say to you, I am the door of the sheep. All who came before Me are thieves and robbers, but the sheep did not hear them. I am the door; if anyone enters through Me, he will be saved, and will go in and out and find pasture. The thief comes only to steal and kill and destroy; I came that they may

have life, and have it abundantly. I am the good shepherd; the good shepherd lays down His life for the sheep.

We are the sheep Jesus speaks of, and we're offered safety and protection by the great Shepherd who is able to guard both our hearts and our lives.

In this story, the word used for "thieves" is *kleptes*—those who steal by means of a carefully executed plan. Whereas the word for "robbers" is *lestes*—those who use violence to get what they want. We need to be on the lookout for both. I've seen both operate in the Christian world with disastrous and tragic consequences.

You may not remember the definitions and distinctions between these two Greek words, but you do need to remember that your Shepherd is watching over His flock. He is standing guard at the gate, and He is willing to lay down His life to defend His own. When the Lord talked about the sheep hearing His voice, He was saying they could distinguish between the voice of their Shepherd, other shepherds and imposters. One of my great fears for the body of Christ today is that we don't know how to discern the true voice of God from an impersonator. The key is the Word of God and the Spirit of God bearing witness to the voice. God does not speak in a vacuum or guide out of context of the revelation of Himself in the Scriptures.

Jesus referred to Himself as the Good Shepherd (John 10:11, 14), and He spoke of laying down His life for His sheep (10:11, 15, 17–18). Christ protects His fold. He is our Shepherd, and we are His sheep. We understand that Christ took on the thief of death and laid down His life to pay the price for our sin—overcoming the world, the flesh and the devil.

Jesus both guards the door and *is* the door since He is both our Shepherd and the only way to salvation. Robertson writes, "One can call this narrow intolerance, if he will, but it is the narrowness of truth. If Jesus is the Son of God sent to earth for our salvation, He is the only way."[19] Jesus said, "If anyone enters though Me, he will be saved." This word is what keeps us safe and secure. We can rest in our Savior.

Christ is the only door, the only way and the only truth. All other doors, all other ways and all other so-called truths lead to destruction. Thieves, wolves and robbers can only be successful if you aren't tuned in to the voice of the Shepherd. You can take risks and leave your heart unguarded and vulnerable. Are you staying safely within the fold of God's flock, or are you placing yourself in danger by wandering away from His pasture?

Jesus also said that if anyone enters through Him, he will "go in and out and find pasture." Not only do we find salvation in Christ, but we're also given the nourishment we need to maintain a healthy Christian life. He enriches every aspect of our lives.

In earlier chapters we looked at the necessity for and the components of an upgraded life, but these mean nothing unless we understand and appropriate the core message of the gospel, which hinges on Christ's death and resurrection. Why did He die for us, and what do we do with this understanding? And, almost as importantly, why does He refer to us as woolly farm animals?

Let's take a walk through Scripture. Remember that normally when we're compared to animals (sheep, donkeys, heifers, etc.) in the Scriptures, it's not complimentary. Why not? It's a reminder that we are dumb like sheep, stubborn like donkeys and want to walk in ruts like an old heifer. Don't be offended by this, but learn from it.

ACCEPT IT—YOU'RE A SHEEP

Referring to the church as God's flock is no new concept. The Old Testament is littered with comparisons to sheepherding.

And even though we're blessed to live under a new covenant in Christ, we're still compared to sheep. Warren Wiersbe gives five reasons why Christ uses the imagery of sheep to refer to the saints:

1. *Sheep are "clean" animals.* (See Leviticus 11:1–8.) In the Old Testament God declared sheep clean and acceptable to His people because they're cloven-footed, cud-chewing animals. Believers are compared to sheep—not some "detestable" animal—so we never have to be separated from the Lord.

2. *Sheep need a shepherd.* Sheep need someone to guide them, protect them and keep them out of trouble. The English word "pastor" comes from the Latin word for shepherd, which is equivalent to an elder, bishop or overseer. The pastor of a church should care for the flock of his church just as Christ cares for us—leading us in the direction we should go. Unless we follow our Shepherd, we'll wander off His path.

3. *Sheep know their shepherd.* Shepherds are intimately acquainted with their sheep. They know their names and their habits. We are not numbers or statistics but living beings who are known and loved by God.

4. *Sheep are useful animals.* Shepherds didn't lead their sheep to slaughter. Rather, they protected them, keeping them for their coats. The sheep were sacrificed at some of Israel's feasts and observances (such as Passover), but for the most part their function was to supply wool. As Christ's sheep, Jesus has every right to expect us to be useful and productive for Him. We are to be living sacrifices, willing to give whatever He asks of us.

5. *Sheep flock together.* Goats tend to scatter, but sheep want to be with other sheep. Similarly, true believers want to be with other believers.

Solely looking at this list, it might be easy to get a big head about being a sheep. They sound like docile, likable creatures. But sheep are actually pretty weak and have limited intelligence. They have to be led to food, and they'll get into trouble if left to wander. They're easily frightened and have no way of defending themselves. Max Lucado writes,

> Sheep aren't smart. They tend to wander into running creeks for water, then their wool grows heavy and they drown. They need a shepherd to lead them to still waters. They have no natural defense—no claws, no horns, no fangs. They are helpless. Sheep need a shepherd with a "rod and a staff" to protect them. They have no sense of direction. They need someone to lead them "in paths of righteousness."[20]

We don't like admitting that we're weak, dependent, wandering sheep, but it's the truth. Jesus reminds us that we're completely unable both to save ourselves and to keep ourselves saved. We are absolutely dependent on our Shepherd. Warren Wiersbe teaches,

> We are sinners by choice and by nature. Like sheep, we are born with a nature that prompts us to go astray and like sheep we foolishly decide to go our own way. By nature we are born children of wrath (Eph 2:3) and by choice we become children of disobedience (2:2). Under the Law of Moses, the sheep died for the shepherd; but under grace, the Good Shepherd died for the sheep (John 10:1–18). [21]

Here's why recognizing that we're helpless apart from the Lord is important: as long as I still think I'm really *something*, Christ can't be my everything. My self-sufficiency and my strengths are of no help to God. It's only when I recognize that I have nothing to offer of my own merit that He can show off His full glory in a situation.

Sheep are also prone to wander. America is full of individualistic people. We like doing things in our own power. We have a hard time with words like "submission" and "surrender." Why?

They demand dying to self. I've met enough people with this spirit in the church whose title song is Frank Sinatra's, "I did it *my way*." We may think this type of living brings freedom, but it actually puts us on paths where the Enemy can ensnare and devour us. Drifting never leads to deeper discipleship.

Because we wander and transgress like dumb sheep, our Great Shepherd has to step in to save us from ourselves. Sheep need a shepherd; sinners need a Savior. Christ the Shepherd was also the sacrificial Lamb. Isaiah 53:7 says the Messiah "was oppressed and He was afflicted, yet He did not open His mouth; like a lamb that is led to slaughter, and like a sheep that is silent before its shearers." Jesus is called "the Lamb" twenty-eight times in Revelation. He is "the Lamb of God who takes away the sin of the world" (John 1:29). Do you see the significance? Christ, the holy Shepherd, became a sacrificial Lamb. Only because of His sacrifice can we enjoy the benefits of being the sheep of His pasture.

Our response to being cared for as God's flock should be worship. The psalmist praised God for being the Good Shepherd:

Know that the Lord Himself is God;
It is He who has made us, and not we ourselves;
We are His people and the sheep of His pasture.
Enter His gates with thanksgiving
And His courts with praise.
Give thanks to Him, bless His name.
For the Lord is good; His lovingkindness is everlasting
And His faithfulness to all generations. (100:3–5)

We should be filled with thanksgiving for who the Lord is and all He has done!

SHEEP NEED A SHEPHERD

While talking about shepherds and sheep might not be a hot topic in today's technology-driven world, it is scriptural. Even though Ephesus was an urban center, Paul reminded the church leaders that they were ministering to God's sheep. In Acts 20:28 he charged them, "Keep watch over yourselves and all the flock of which the Holy Spirit has made you overseers."

In America we probably know more about cowboys than shepherds thanks to old Western movies and the popularity of characters like John Wayne. But in the first century, shepherds were much more prevalent, and we can't compare their role to that of cowherds. Shepherds love their sheep whereas cowboys drive their herds. Shepherds lead their sheep to be shorn whereas cowboys lead their cows to be slaughtered. Shepherds know the names of each sheep whereas cowboys brand their cows with numbers. Shepherds call their sheep by name whereas cowboys yell, whoop and holler. We don't need individualistic, proud cowboys; we need one Good Shepherd.

Psalm 80:1 refers to Jehovah as the "Shepherd of Israel," and when God delivered the Israelites from bondage, "He led forth His own people like sheep and guided them in the wilderness like a flock" (78:52). Jeremiah condemned the religious and political leaders who were destroying the flock of God, and, referring to the Babylonian captivity, he warned, "the LORD's flock will be taken captive" (13:17).

Christ frequently referenced Himself as being our Shepherd. In John 10:11–15 Jesus asserted,

> I am the good shepherd; the good shepherd lays down His life for the sheep. He who is a hired hand, and not a shepherd, who is not the owner of the sheep, sees the wolf coming, and leaves the sheep and flees, and the wolf snatches them and scatters them. He flees because he is a hired hand and is not concerned about the sheep. I am the good shepherd, and I know My own and My own know Me, even as the Father knows Me and I know the Father; and I lay down My life for the sheep.

It's significant that Christ stresses this aspect of His nature. Because of the Lord's pastoral caretaking, we are protected and valued. We can rest in His care. When we truly understand what it means to be a sheep in God's flock, we move into a new level of intimacy with the Great Shepherd.

There are three central aspects to Christ's Shepherd-hood: He is the Good Shepherd who died for His sheep (John 10:11, 15–16, 18); He is the Great Shepherd who lives to protect His sheep (Heb. 13:20–21); He is the Chief Shepherd who will return for His sheep (1 Pet. 5:1–4).

The psalmist, himself a shepherd, celebrated each of these three aspects. Psalm 22 describes the Good Shepherd who gave His life for His sheep. Psalm 23 describes the Great Shepherd who provides and protects the sheep "all the days of [our lives]." Psalm 24 describes the Chief Shepherd who will defeat His enemies and reward His people.

Several years ago I read a magazine article by a prominent pastor in America who is followed by millions and who considers himself a role model for young pastors. In effect he said that if Jesus were alive today, He wouldn't call Himself a Shepherd but a CEO. First, I was furious at the arrogance of such a statement. Second, I was stunned by his complete lack of biblical understanding of what a shepherd does. What troubled me even more is how many thousands of leaders might have read that and never had a check in their own spirits about how unbiblical such a view of pastoring is. CEOs only look at the bottom line, numbers and profits; real shepherds care about their sheep.

Being a part of the Lord's flock is valuable for many reasons. *First, the Shepherd knows where our needs can be met.* He knows how to find supply enough for the entire flock to not only survive but to prosper. The psalmist started Psalm 23 with, "The Lord is my shepherd, I shall not want." To "not want" is to be content. We have Christ watching over us, so we have no need to fear because He is our constant and complete supply. He is our source of peace and satisfaction.

Our Shepherd offers us abundant life in Him. Unfortunately, many preachers today teach that the abundant life is the life of painless prosperity. This sounds good, but you can't remove the call to suffer for the cause of the gospel.

So what is the abundant life? The English word "abundance" comes from two Latin words meaning "to rise in waves" and "to overflow." Picture a tide coming in, advancing up the shore. The abundant life is the life that overflows with Christ. The waters of serving Him and loving Him should never recede because He offers us everything necessary to sustain the flow.

Second, the Shepherd knows how to protect us from all evil. Shepherds in the Middle East are aware of all types of danger. They know how to defend against predators, and they know where to place their sheep when flash floods come in the winter. There may be storms and crises, but sheep who take refuge in the Shepherd will find the security they long for.

Third, the Shepherd leads us to contentment. This means something slightly different for us than for literal sheep. By "contentment," I'm not necessarily talking about a happy, easy existence. God's abundant life comes with the assurance that He is able to meet every need and to overcome every crisis. Strong faith comes through testing. Will you abide in the Lord even when danger surrounds you? The psalmist wrote, "Even though I walk through the valley of the shadow of death, I fear no evil for You are with me; Your rod and Your staff, they comfort me" (23:4).

Psalm 23:2–3 reads, "He makes me lie down in green pastures; He leads me beside quiet waters. [My source of satisfaction.] He restores my soul; He guides me in the paths of righteousness For

His name's sake. [My strength and guide.]" The phrase "He makes me lie down" is significant. Phillip Keller explains why:

> It is almost impossible for them [sheep] to be made to lie down unless four requirements are met. Owing to their timidity they refuse to lie down unless they are free of all fear. Because of the social behavior within a flock, sheep will not lie down unless they are free from friction with others of their kind. If torment-ed by flies or parasites, sheep will not lie down. . . . Lastly, sheep will not lie down as long as they feel in need of finding food. They must be free from hunger. [22]

Only our Great Shepherd is capable of providing us with what we need to fully rest—freedom from fear, stress, aggravation and hunger. This is true for us now, and it will be true for us eternally. Revelation 7:16–17 teaches, "They will hunger no longer, nor thirst anymore; nor will the sun beat down on them, nor any heat; for the Lamb in the center of the throne will be their shepherd, and will guide them to springs of the water of life; and God will wipe every tear from their eyes."

The Lord is able to do abundantly more than we can think to ask. He functions far above our imaginations, and He works His great power in and through us. Our lives are complete in Him; He is our fullness. Our greatest honor and our greatest challenge is to be the faithful sheep of His flock.

KNOWING THE SHEPHERD

Because our Shepherd is our door to salvation and security and our access to freedom and the abundant life, our Enemy has to work to steal us away. Never forget that the devil and his forces are alive and active in our world.

Our response to the Enemy's attacks is important. First, we must distinguish between the one true Shepherd and the false shepherds. Today we have a lot of preachers and religious leaders whose only agenda is to make themselves look good. Rather than seeking to accurately teach God's Word for the advancement of His kingdom, these hustlers try to gain a following through deception and manipulation.

John 10:1 says, "He who does not enter by the door into the fold of the sheep, but climbs up some other way, he is a thief and a robber." Those intent on deception seek to avoid detection. Satan is a master of misrepresentation. His false shepherds appeal to our flesh by offering a fake version of the gospel that demands nothing—a faith that tries to make God our servant.

In our build-your-own-religion culture, people try to make Jesus into whomever they want Him to be. Ray Stedman asserts, "Today there are many false teachers presenting false views of Jesus. Many people ask, 'Who is the true Jesus? Who is the true Shepherd of the sheep?' There is the Jesus of the Moonies, the Jesus of the Jehovah's Witnesses, the Jesus of the Christian Scientists, the Jesus of the Mormons, the Jesus of the New Age, the Jesus of a thousand bizarre cults and philosophies."[23]

So how do we accurately identify Jesus, our true Shepherd? There are several things about Him that make Him the One.

1. *Jesus can identify His own sheep.* John 10:3 says, "He calls His own sheep by name and leads them out." When the sheep distinguish their Shepherd's voice among the others, it's not simply because He's yelling the loudest. They're attentive to His call because they recognize His voice and because He *calls them by name.* Christ knows us intimately—down to the tiniest detail—and cares for us in the exact ways we need Him to (see Luke 12:6–7).

2. *Jesus is the only gate.* Jesus and Jesus alone fulfilled every Old Testament prophecy about the Messiah. Therefore He is the only way to eternal, abundant life. Of course, when Christ referred to Himself as the gate, He was talking about more than just the gate to salvation. The phrase He used in verse 9, "go in

and out," is a figurative expression for living life. We all need to live in Christ. The Greek word for "shepherd" is *poimen*, which is derived from the root meaning "to protect." We're secure when we trust that Christ has given us access to His kingdom.

3. *Jesus leads and guides His sheep.* Christ isn't absent from us, sitting at a gate somewhere far away, contemplating things and staring off into space. No, He is our ever-present Shepherd. He provides His sheep everything they needed for their journey, and His Spirit leads us in paths of righteousness. Any teaching or doctrine that does not teach us to be more holy—more like Jesus—is not the true voice of our Shepherd.

4. *Jesus speaks to our hearts, and the Holy Spirit bears witness.* In the Middle East shepherds drive their flocks into a central sheepfold—some protected enclosure—every evening. As many as half a dozen flocks might be contained in one fold. In the morning each shepherd returns to claim his sheep, and the sheep know their individual shepherd's voice. Similarly, when you're walking in the Spirit, sometimes you will hear something taught that doesn't ring true to you. That's Christ's Spirit telling you, "That person isn't speaking My truth." Jesus never promised prosperity for believers, healing for everyone or constant happiness. Don't listen or accept anything that contradicts biblical teaching. Instead, run away from falsehood like the robber of joy and security that it is!

Watch Out for Thieves and Robbers!

Christ contrasted Himself with His predecessors: "All who came before Me are thieves and robbers" (10:8). He didn't refer to the patriarchs of the faith but to false teachers—the Pharisees and scribes who placed heavy, ungodly burdens on the people. He talked about the false prophets who took advantage of the flock through their status and deception. These types of "thieves and robbers" still exist in the church today—telling people what they want to hear and creating bizarre cults for their own glorification.

Satan is the force behind all the thieves and robbers who seek to steal and destroy.

1. *He is the accuser of the brethren.* Revelation 12:10 teaches that the "accuser of the brethren"—the devil—will be cast down, which means that he's currently on the prowl, getting us into trouble. In First Peter 5:8 Satan is compared to "a roaring lion, seeking someone to devour." He's looking for folks he can catch off guard and take down.

2. *He's the adversary.* Mark 8:33 tells us that the devil is violently opposed to the rule of God. He resists God's plan and purposes. Therefore, he is our Enemy. First Peter 5:8 actually refers to Satan as "Your adversary, the devil."

3. *He's the father of lies.* In John 8:42–45 Jesus explained that the devil is the enemy of truth. Satan is the author of confusion; he is always seeking to deceive and can never be trusted.

4. *He is the prince of this world.* Satan actually has a great deal of power in the secular realm. One day this will be revoked, but for now he is free to rule in the earth (John 12:31; 14:30). He seeks to influence, intimidate and impress. Don't let yourself be swayed by his charm.

5. *He is the evil one.* Satan is opposed to all that is good (John 17:15), and he perverts all that is true and holy.

Satan is always up to no good. It's important to discern his strategy so we aren't deceived. Jesus said anyone who tried to enter the kingdom any other way than through the gate was a thief and a robber. Satan and his cronies are continually on the lookout for ways to circumvent God's laws, and they present these alternatives to God's commands in a tempting fashion. Let's look at a few key facets of the evil one's attacks.

Satan pushes for the denial of Christ. Because the devil is opposed to all the things of God, he wasn't pleased about Christ being sent to redeem humanity and reconcile us to God. Therefore, he works to make us reject Christ. The fruits of his efforts are seen in the reactions of the Pharisees to Jesus in the Gospel of John: "Some of the Pharisees were saying, 'This man is not from God, because He does not keep the Sabbath . . . We know that God has spoken to Moses, but as for this man, we do not know where He is from'" (9:16, 29).

Satan urges the rejection of Christ as Messiah. When the parents of the blind man Jesus healed were asked about what had happened, they responded hesitantly "because they were afraid of the Jews, for already the Jews had decided that anyone who acknowledged that Jesus was the Christ would be put out of the synagogue" (John 9:22). Christ is deity, and He died to save us. Anyone who says differently is buying into Satan's lie.

Satan promotes blasphemy. The word "blasphemy" is a transliteration of a Greek word that means "to speak harm." We blaspheme when we disrespect God's character by having a negative, malicious attitude or by twisting Christ's teachings for our own benefit. The Sanhedrin accused Jesus of blasphemy for asserting His divine sonship (Mark 2:7), but the real blasphemers are those who deny Him as the Messiah.

Satan blinds people's minds to the truth. There's a pattern to the way the devil operates: he always seeks to lead us away from Christ. In some cases this involves deceiving believers; in others, it involves attempting to lead unbelievers astray. "And even if our gospel is veiled, it is veiled to those who are perishing, in whose case *the god of this world has blinded the minds of the unbelieving* so that they might not see the light of the gospel of the glory of Christ, who is the image of God" (2 Cor. 4:3–4).

Satan blinds people to their own blindness. Once Satan has deceived someone, he works to keep that person from recognizing their blindness to the truth. In John 9:39–41 Jesus condemned the Pharisees for their blindness. They were blind because they refused to see the Light standing before them and believe in Him. Satan blinded them by their own self-righteousness and false interpretation of the Word. Although they claimed to have spiritual sight, their sinful pride in their own traditions led them to refuse Christ.

Satan offers alternatives to the narrow way. Satan and his prophets try to add false doctrine to the simple gospel message. They deny the cross and the blood of the true Shepherd that was shed for us. Seeking to divide and destroy, the devil tempts us to follow broader, easier paths. False prophets tell us we can think whatever we want to think and believe whatever we want to believe as long as we're "good people." Christ didn't die for good people (Mark 2:17). He died for sinners who acknowledge their desperate need for Him and who are willing to sacrifice to follow Him.

Satan's powers of manipulation and trickery are evident throughout the ages. The Jewish people dealt with kings who ruled for their own pleasure, false prophets who said what carnal people wanted to hear and Pharisees who padded their pockets. Not much has changed since then. We will always have corrupt, false teachers who tickle people's ears. Thieves and robbers are still among us.

What do we do when we're surrounded by these types of people? Exactly what the sheep in Christ's analogy did—trust the Shepherd. Your responsibility is to discern His voice and follow Him—no matter what the masses say.

The key to averting the destructive attacks of the Enemy is to remain intimately connected to the Lord.

INTIMACY DESIRED, BUT DERAILED

Do you desire intimacy with God yet feel like you just can't get there? What's keeping you from knowing Jesus as the lover of your soul?

Because we are like sheep, we desire closeness with a shepherd. We need someone who knows us best and loves us still. Think about it—the main reason kids give in to peer pressure is because of their desire to fit in and be accepted as part of a gang or group. That need to belong follows us to adulthood.

We also long for significance. We want to matter, and we recognize that we *do* matter to Christ. Our Good Shepherd calls us by name and cares for us. He wipes away our sins, tears and pain. We need forgiveness, and He offers freedom from guilt and feelings of inadequacy.

A desire for intimacy is the natural response when we learn about the One who loves us unconditionally and offers us security, peace, joy and abundant life. So why does this closeness sometimes elude us?

If you're honest with yourself, what would you say your priorities are? Look at your agenda if you need help; the way you spend your time reflects what you consider important. Is your schedule centered on getting closer to God and doing His work? If not, it may be time for a reevaluation.

Three major things separate us from our loving Creator.

1. *Apathy of the heart.* We find it easy to be passionate—almost to the point of worship—about our kids, job, money, hobbies and Alma Mater, but we often fail to actively seek God. We drift along, content to live with a *que sera, sera* attitude. Like Paul wrote in Romans 3:9, "There is no one who seeks God." As discussed in chapter 3, such apathy allows our relationship with the Lord to deteriorate.

2. *Autonomy of the "old man."* Second Timothy 3:2 de-

scribes men as "lovers of self." Our sinful nature tells us we are our highest priority. We tend to place our own individual desires above others'—including God's.

Even Christians seem to find it inconvenient to spend time with God. Wednesday after Wednesday I watch parents drop their kids off at church. Rather than taking advantage of our discipleship classes designed to help them grow in their walk with the Lord, they use the "free time" to go shopping or out to eat. And I'm not trying to come down hard on my congregation. The truth is that the general trend for Americans is to put their personal interests first. Only when we prioritize the Lord will we be free from the tyranny of what we think is urgent now.

3. *Aspirations of the flesh.* As fallen beings, we are lovers of pleasure and money, and those fleshly desires die hard. It's difficult to walk away from what the world offers—even though we realize it's infinitely inferior to what God has promised His followers.

Here's the good news—even though the things that hold us back from God may seem like big stumbling blocks to us, God is greater. We have to choose to turn over our selfish desires and draw closer to Him. When we do, He'll draw near to us.

INTIMACY DISCOVERED AND DEVELOPED

God knows you inside and out, and He loves you more fully than anyone else ever could. He is both the Creator of the universe and your Wonderful Counselor. So if there's a problem with intimacy, it's not on God's side.

Men especially seem to have a difficult time with intimacy. We're afraid that worshiping God will somehow make us less of a man when actually the best thing we can do is fall on our knees before God. David was a strong man who had a deep connection with God. He wrote, "You scrutinize my path and my lying down, and are intimately acquainted with all my ways. Even before there is a word on my tongue, behold, O Lord, You know it all" (139:3–4).

The word "scrutinize" here is the same term used to describe digging deep into a mine, exploring a land or investigating a legal case. God isn't just aware of you and the circumstances that affect you—He's actively involved in knowing everything about you. Take a moment to let that sink in. When you recognize the weight of who God is and yet how much He loves you, your response should be to draw closer to Him.

God knows your every thought, word and motive. Hebrews 4:13 says, "Nothing in all creation is hidden from God's sight. Everything is uncovered and laid bare before the eyes of him to whom we must give account" (NIV).

You don't have to worry about coming to Him and telling Him things because He already knows it all. This shouldn't be disconcerting but rather freeing because it means that God knows what's best for us. He knows us and loves us still.

Even when we're weak, demanding infants, God shows infinite care for us. Writing to God, Max Lucado drives home this point:

> We ignore the Word you sent us. We killed the Son you became. We are spoiled babies who take and kick and pout and blaspheme. You have every reason to abandon us.
>
> Father your love never ceases. Never. Though we spurn you, ignore you, disobey you, you will not change. Our evil cannot diminish your love. Our goodness cannot increase it. Our faith does not earn it any more than our stupidity jeopardizes it. You don't love us less if we fail. You don't love us more if we succeed. Your love never ceases.
>
> God's love is not human. His love is not normal. His love sees your sin and loves you still. Does he approve of your error?

No. Do you need to repent? Yes. But do you repent for His sake or yours? Yours. His ego needs no apology. His love needs no bolstering.

And he could not love you more than he does right now.[24]

Nothing about us was worth dying for or saving, but Jesus paid the price anyway—that's how deep His love for us is. If you want to develop an intimate relationship with Him, then listen when He speaks (John 10:3), follow where He leads (10:4), come when He says come (10:9), go when He says go (10:9), accept what He provides (10:9) and obey when He commands you to come out of your comfort zone (10:4).

We can show love to others only because Christ loved us first. God is good, and His love endures forever (Ps. 136:1). Therefore we can trust Him with our lives. Seek the Lord. Pray for Him to move in a mighty way in your life. Fall before His throne.

Even though you're a lowly sheep, your Shepherd cares for you. Don't miss your chance to bask in the shelter of His fold, safe from the thieves and robbers who will try to steal you or lead you astray. Seek God, and you'll find more and more of Him!

Listen, my fellow sheep. The Shepherd is demanding your attention.

RESTING IN THE FATHER

I AM NOT a prosperity gospel preacher. I'm not a "health and wealth" guy. I believe the Scriptures tell us that in this world we will have persecution and suffering. But, for the sake of argument, what would you say if I told you I had a cure for all your anxieties? What if I promised you I could take away all your concerns? What if I said I could *guarantee* victory in every area of your life?

You might be skeptical . . . and you should be. I can't offer these things. But Christ can. Jesus is the answer to every situation, and He longs to be your Prince of Peace.

However, victory might not always feel like victory. The "upgraded life" often appears difficult to our worldly sensibilities. I'm editing this chapter just having left the CCU at our local hospital where a longtime member of my prayer team and a leader in our church is struggling to survive. Sitting in the room with him, his wife and I discussed how God knows our days. There was victory in the air—even in a room filled with the hubbub of tubes, monitors and nurses coming in and out. There was assurance in the midst of an anxious time. That's a real upgrade. Only God can be your peace through a rough storm.

A few weeks ago I was flying to speak in another state. Because I travel so much, I got a free upgrade to first class. I was comfortable in the front row with plenty of legroom. Of course that didn't matter much when we hit a horrendous storm. Lightening popped like fireworks. The plane bounced around, and people were nauseated. It wasn't a smooth flight, but we survived. The lady sitting beside me had wine and a few other mixed drinks, and she still about lost it. I found peace through prayer. In the anxious moments of life, the refreshing presence of Christ, the Living Water, is more soothing than any drink man can offer. Christ offers assurance and hope at every stage of our journey.

Over the course of the past eight chapters, we've looked at the requirements for an upgraded life as well as the things that can hinder the workings of the Holy Spirit. You've probably heard many of these teachings before, but you can know something to be true yet fail to apply it to your life. Are you appropriating and applying what you know or what you've been reading? Now that you understand the components of an upgraded life, it's time to apply them.

Upgrades come with a price, but they also offer a life of rest. When we trust the Lord's promises and rely on Jesus, we find relaxation and pure joy. In Matthew 11:28–30 Jesus offers, "Come to Me, all who are weary and heavy-laden, and I will give you rest. Take My yoke upon you and learn from Me, for I am gentle and humble in heart, and you will find rest for your souls. For My yoke is easy and My burden is light."

Christ gives three simple commands: come, take, learn. When you come before Him and partake of His wisdom and strength, you will learn how to rest in Him. This is the beauty of an upgraded life—it involves the most difficult sacrifices, the strongest trust and the greatest rewards.

WHAT KIND OF DISCIPLE ARE YOU?

Before delving into the significance of Christ's words in Matthew 11, I want to give you some context. Prior to His death on the cross, Christ taught His disciples what being a true follower meant. He gave them several commands: fear Me (10:28), confess Me (10:32), love Me (10:37), follow Me (10:38) and die for Me (10:39). This is all-out discipleship. Following these commands will lead you to closer fellowship with Jesus.

Unfortunately, we don't always respond to the Lord in the most ideal ways. During Christ's short time on earth, He was rejected again and again. Overall there were four main ways in which people reacted to Jesus.[25]

First, some were *concerned* (Matt. 11:1–15). John the Baptist represents this group. When things weren't going well, he questioned Christ. But Jesus didn't rebuke John for his honest concerns. Through John's example we see that it's okay to doubt sometimes—as long as you go to the right Person for the answer.

Second, some were *critical* (11:16–19). There will always be religious people who don't understand true faith in Christ and who never take advantage of the life that Christ offers. Don't be flippant, critical and sarcastic like these.

Third, some were *careless* (11:20–24). This is a sad section of Scripture because it speaks of people who saw the light yet chose to walk in darkness. Jesus rebuked the unrepentant cities and pronounced judgment over them. We've been privileged to hear the good news, and now we need to respond to its call. Because we know the truth, we're accountable for what we've heard.

Fourth, some were *childlike* (11:25–30). Christ wants us to approach Him with pure, unadulterated love and faith. Later in the book of Matthew, Jesus told His disciples, "Do not hinder [the children] from coming to Me; for the kingdom of heaven belongs to such as these" (19:14). It's simple—we need to trust the Lord, no more and no less. He knows what is best for us now and forever.

What is your response to Christ? Do you name Him Lord and Savior, or do you criticize His teachings and doubt His authenticity as the Messiah?

Jesus's invitation of freedom—first offered over 2,000 years ago—is still valid today. In Matthew 11 Christ offered a life of liberty. There are only ten recorded prayers of Jesus in this Gospel, and 11:25 is one of the first. In it Jesus made a clear claim of divinity. Then in verse 27 He declared a revelation, which led to His invitation for His followers to live in freedom in Him (11:28–30).

You may have said that you've never heard God speak to you, but He is speaking in these short verses. He is Lord, and He is trustworthy, and His call is, "Come to Me!" Jesus says that no matter what you're going through, no matter what problems you're facing—He will meet you at your point of need. When you feel worn out, frustrated and tired, He will give you rest. He has the power to transform your life.

Christ gives us three commands to build our lives around. If you act on these words, you will be transformed and will experience true peace and joy. To be more like a child, growing in your Father's care, follow Jesus's instructions: come, take and learn.

COME

I was the sole heir of my parents' estate. I don't have any

brothers or sisters. My dad used to say to me, "At least you won't have to fight anyone over the will." Of course, they didn't have much, but all they had came to me as their son and heir. Their will was legal and binding. But the offer of Jesus is greater than a legal contract—it is a loving invitation.

Jesus offers salvation for the lost—yet many reject His call to come. He offers a way of life to the saved that is beyond what man can do on his own. The problem is sometimes we ignore the invitation.

The path of least resistance will come to a dead end, robbing you of a godly legacy. Christianity is not a faith for those who want to dwell in their own comfort zones. It stretches you and challenges you to be like the One who has called you to follow Him.

Christ's words "come to me" are a call to holiness (because He is holy) and to hope (for He is the only hope of man). The call doesn't contain any qualifiers. Christ didn't say, "Come to Me if it's convenient for you" or "Come to Me if your peers approve" or "Come to Me if it fits into your busy schedule." He just told us to come to the Holy One, the spotless Lamb, the Son of God.

Also note that Christ didn't say, "Come and be religious." His invitation is to a personal, intimate relationship with Him. You can either accept this invitation or refuse it—but you will never find rest until you obey His call.

The One you are coming to is "gentle and humble" (11:29). Jesus doesn't just *act* humble; it's His very nature. He wants to build you up. When Christ addresses, "all who are weary and heavy-laden," He's talking about most of us. We all get beat down by life and feel burdened by toils, troubles and tribulations. Nothing in this world offers freedom from such problems. Only Jesus can offer rest from guilt, fear and wearying situations.

Christ's original audience in Matthew was comprised of impoverished agricultural workers who faced long, hard days. They were frequently overtaxed and were constantly reminded that they were peons in the Roman Empire. On top of economic and political burdens, they were further stressed with endless religious rules and regulations instituted by the Pharisees. Jesus said, "They bind heavy burdens, hard to bear, and lay them on men's shoulders" (Matt 23:4). Our burdens, even in tough economic times, are nothing compared to the burdens these folks faced.

Just as we struggle with problems today, the people Jesus initially spoke to faced opposition and difficulty at every turn. But Jesus said, "I've come to help."

I imagine that some of those listening to Christ responded, "Rest?! Who is this guy kidding? He must have no idea what we're dealing with if He thinks He can free us from all of it." You may be thinking the same thing—*How can I rest when my to-do list is a mile long, and I don't even have the time to look at it because I'm busy working just to put food on the table and keep a roof over my family's head?*

The answer is that you can't afford *not* to rest because Jesus told you to rest in Him. Christ didn't say you'd never have pains and problems in the physical realm. What He did promise was that He could give you rest for your soul.

Several years ago I founded the ReFRESH® Conference on revival and spiritual awakening. Currently we have two conferences a year—one at the church I pastor and another in the mountains of Tennessee. We're planning to add others over the next few years because we've seen such a need. Every year pastors and lay leaders roll into town exhausted and ready to quit, wearied and longing for relief. I often say, "You guys have come in on four flat tires with a letter of resignation in your hand. My hope and prayer is that before this conference is over, you'll choose to stay in the battle. To do that you need to understand the power of the Holy Spirit and the walk of faith."

I know that you want to feel refreshed and rejuvenated. Jesus offers peace of mind and spiritual peace—in the midst of the world's hectic demands.

TAKE

The next step isn't going to sound very restful. After Christ calls us to come to Him, He says, "Take My yoke upon you." Often when I preach this passage, I take a yoke with me. If you don't know what one looks like, do an image search online; seeing a yoke gives you a good idea of how it works.

One of the most common metaphors used in biblical times was that of the yoke, which indicated submission to an occupation or obligation. But Jesus didn't say He'd force us to work for Him. Instead, He told us to take the yoke by a free and deliberate choice. You can't get into a yoke without putting your head down, which is an act of humble surrender.

It's important to realize that Christ didn't offer us a pillow or a recliner—He offers a yoke. Wearing a yoke is not a way to get out of work. Wearing a yoke does not conjure up images of a relaxing vacation far away from everything that stresses us. But wearing a yoke makes our burden lighter.

Do you see what Jesus suggested in Matthew 11? He said, "If you'll yoke up with Me, we'll do this together. We'll face life side by side. I'm in this with you—if you'll bow down and accept this yoke." When Christ said His "yoke is easy," He meant that it fits well. Back in the day, yokes were tailor-made for each ox. Similarly, Jesus knows exactly what you can bear and the best way for you to bear it. Christ told us His burden is light, which means it's easy to carry. We aren't being driven by a malicious owner but by a gracious Lord who loves us.

Being yoked to Christ means we can't run ahead of Him or fall behind His purposes—we have to walk in step with Him. This is the life of surrender. Service to others and to the Lord is only a burden when we try to do it on our own.

The fact that Jesus calls it *His* yoke is significant. It means that He gets to set the direction and the pace of your life. If you resist His leadership and pull against Him, the yoke will become an added burden. Your goal should be to do Christ's work, not your own. The most significant thing you can do in your life is to learn how to follow Christ.

LEARN

Learning from Christ is the third component of His command. Jesus always has something new to teach us. We never graduate from His school of discipleship.

Christ didn't tell the early church to learn from the traditions of the rabbis. Rather, He told them to learn from Him. As the Way, the Truth and the Life, Jesus is both the Teacher and the Lesson to be learned. He did what He taught, and He taught what He did.

Our hope does not come from keeping rules but from our relationship with Christ. We're incapable of living according to His will on our own, but He never asked us to. He wants to live His life through us.

I ran across a great list a few years ago containing several things we need to learn from our Teacher. (I've since forgotten the source, but not the truth contained in it.)

1. *We need to learn His mind.* "Let this mind be in you which was in Christ Jesus" (Phil. 2:5).
2. *We need to learn His lifestyle.* "[Jesus] emptied Himself, taking the form of a bond-servant" (Phil. 2:6–7).
3. *We need to learn His humility.* "[Christ] humbled Him-

self by becoming obedient to the point of death, even death on a cross" (Phil. 2:8).

4. *We need to learn His heart.* Jesus wept over Jerusalem (Luke 19:41). He died for the lost (1 Pet. 2:24), and He commissioned us to care for one another (John 13:34).

5. *We need to learn to exhibit the fruit of the Spirit* (as listed in Galatians 5:22–23). "Now those who belong to Christ Jesus have crucified the flesh with its passions and desires" (Gal. 5:24).

6. *We need to learn to discipline our lives.* As Christ's disciples, we need to daily sit at His feet in personal Bible study, in worship, in prayer and in forgiveness of others.

Because of our Teacher, we know how to live. We are free in His yoke. If you look at the faces of most of the people you meet on the streets, you'll see hopeless eyes. People are burdened and weak. Yet Christ offers liberty. Sometimes we wear ourselves out trying to be good and trying to find God. We get tired of trying to follow religious rules. This isn't the way to God. As W.B. Yeats noted, "Can one reach God by toil? No! He gives Himself to the pure in heart. He asks nothing but our attention."[26]

Jesus loves you and knows what's best for you. When you come to Him, take His yoke and learn from Him, you discover that life's burdens are infinitely lighter. When He says, "You will find rest for your soul," it's a promise. One of the blessings of the upgraded life is freedom and peace in Christ.

What are you waiting for? The process of coming, taking and learning is continuous. There's always more of Christ to find, and He always has more to teach you. He is able and willing to do abundantly more for you than you can imagine. He is all the strength and supply you will ever need. The Shepherd is waiting and calling; Jesus is saying to you now, "Come to Me." Will you?

UPGRADES LEAD TO JOY

I N HIS BOOK *Restoring Your Spiritual Passion*, Gordon MacDonald tells of a traveler who hired natives from the jungles of Africa to carry his supplies. On the first day, they made incredibly good time. But on the second day, the tribesmen refused to move. When the traveler questioned why, they responded that they had gone too fast on the first day and now had to wait for their souls to catch up with their bodies.

While you probably don't worry about physically losing your soul working too hard (nor should you), you might have something to learn from these natives. It's possible to get so caught up in all the things you have to do in a given day that you allow spiritual maturity to take second place to busyness. It's easy to put works before the Word and performance before prayer.

When I was a student pastor, I would talk to the students about the importance of spending time with God. I would tell them, "No Bible, no breakfast." Of course, their comeback was always that they didn't eat breakfast to which I responded, "You probably don't get up in time to have a quiet time either." God has to come first.

As a pastor, I take study sabbaticals to maintain my connection with the Lord. It's possible to fall into patterns in any line of work, and preaching Sunday after Sunday, there's a risk for sermons to become nothing more than rehearsed speeches. Many pastors rehash an old sermon by simply changing the outline—but that's not a fresh word from God. A pastor can't feed his people with stale bread. For a work to be blessed by God, it has to be grounded in Him. I need to preach out of an overflow of God's Spirit—not out of the demand to have a sermon prepared.

Christians often allow "good" to become the enemy of "best"—serving more and enjoying it less. We're busy, but we're barren. Some of us have heard so many sermons and gone to so many Bible studies that we feel as if we should have gained enough knowledge to coast for the rest of our lives. Yet when we're confronted with a spiritual battle, we feel ill-equipped.

It's easier to talk about commitment and passion than to maintain them. We grow weary and want to run from the battle. But God's Word gives us fundamental truths for living the victorious Christian life.

Look at Jesus—He had to start a worldwide ministry in three-and-a-half years with a group of ragtag followers. No church planter would think, "This is the core group that's going to help me reach this city." The disciples were not qualified according to worldly standards. However, Jesus saw something in them and called them.

Christ didn't blog. He didn't have a Facebook page or a Twitter account. Yet His communication was powerful and far-reaching. How did He do it? Well, for starters, He walked a lot, sharing with people and caring for them. Even though He had a great deal to do in a short amount of time, Jesus never seemed to be in a hurry. He was never a slave to the clock, and He never seemed to worry about the size of the crowds around Him.

We live weary lives, running from place to place and stressing over every small setback. We've forgotten what we should remember—Christ is with us, and we can rest in our Prince of Peace. God's promises are not for an elite few but for all who believe and appropriate what He has given us.

Christ in you is what you need to face adversity and opposition. John reminds us,

> Let that abide in you which you heard from the beginning. If what you heard from the beginning abides in you, you also will abide in the Son and in the Father. This is the promise which He Himself made to us: eternal life. These things I have written to you concerning those who are trying to deceive you.[27] As for you, the anointing which you received from Him abides in you, and you have no need for anyone to teach you; but as His anointing teaches you about all things, and is true and is not a lie, and just as it has taught you, you abide in Him. Now, little children, abide in Him, so that when He appears, we may have confidence and not shrink away from Him in shame at His coming. If you know that He is righteous, you know that everyone also who practices righteousness is born of Him. (1 John 2: 24–29)

IT'S ALL ABOUT ABIDING

Victory is not a once-and-for-all change. It's not an emotional surge. There's no five-step plan you can follow. Victory is an active process, and until you come to grips with the fact that it's impossible without Christ, you'll be frustrated and will live at a lower level than God intended.

If you don't grasp the nature of abiding, you won't be able to live on a higher plane. You'll settle instead of soar. Unfortunately, there are teachers who take verses out of context and claim you have to work to earn your salvation. Those teachers are thieves and robbers. They steal your joy and make you live in habitual frustration. They set standards of legalism and performance (trying hard within the flesh) that God never set. This kind of living only leads to frustration—never to contentment, joy, peace or power.

For nearly thirty years, I've been studying Jesus's teachings on abiding. They have revolutionized my life. Truths about abiding are liberating for all who embrace them. To "abide" means to settle down and let Jesus be at home in your heart. Salvation is an inward, permanent experience. Abiding is continuous, and through the Holy Spirit's residing within us, Christ rules our lives.

Don't think that abiding is passive. You still have a part to play. Think of it as heaven's enabling power met with human responsibility. God gives me what I need in order to do what He calls me to do, and I cooperate with Him. First John challenges us to "walk in the same manner as [Christ] walked" (2:6) and to live in the light (2:10). When John tells us, "Let that abide in you which you heard from the beginning" (2:24), he uses the present imperative third-person singular. In other words, he stresses that *we need* to allow the Lord's power to work in and through us *continually*. "Being saved" is not just a decision you made in the past; it has present results.

God is changing you from the inside out. Victory comes when the truth lives in and through you. It's Jesus "in whom are hidden all the treasures of wisdom and knowledge." Because He gave you His Holy Spirit to abide within you and empower you, you have the ability to grow spiritually (1 Pet. 2:1–2), live a pure life (Ps. 119:9–11) and be fruitful (John 15:5).

I see so many believers who are stressed out, anxious and fearful. They seem to live on an emotional edge and have little joy or peace. They are fragile and quickly falter in their faith if something doesn't go their way. But this is not the way God intended us to live!

Do you, as one of Christ's followers, rest in Him? Are you experiencing all He offers by finding your peace in His fullness? Christ abides and dwells within you—are you abiding and dwelling in His victory?

SUSTAINED BY THE SPIRIT

You can't abide in Christ by your own power. He has to be your power source; He is your central resource for this life. The good news is that "you have an anointing from the Holy One" and "the anointing which you received from Him abides in you" (1 John 2:20, 27). The Holy Spirit is within you, and He sustains you so you can enjoy the fullness of your anointing. Some of us are living on the wrong side of Pentecost. I'm not speaking here of gifts or manifestations but of power. We live as if the Spirit has not come or as if His coming wasn't for us but only for the real superstars and saints in the body of Christ. The Spirit came to declare God's truths to every one of us (John 16:14).

The Spirit will help you to discern the truth so no one can lead you astray. Ephesians 5:6 challenges, "Let no one deceive you with empty words," and Second Thessalonians also cautions, "Let no one in any way deceive you." We as believers are under the constant bombardment of deception. For this reason, we can't allow our feelings to determine our actions. Don't confuse emotions and feelings with a deep work of God. And don't confuse the lack of adrenalin with the absence of anointing.

God isn't going to do His deepest work in the shallowest part of our nature. He speaks in a still small voice. He quietly leads and directs, and He trusts us to listen and follow. This is why it's important to be in the Word. You need to know what you believe, and you need to know the truth so those with the Antichrist's spirit in this world cannot deceive you!

Whenever you read the Bible, pray for the Holy Spirit to help you interpret it accurately. As one of my friends says, "The author of the Word is in the room with you." Think about it. The Scriptures are inspired, God-breathed. The author is with you—and actually in you—to guide you into all truth. The Spirit's roles of conviction, guidance, discernment and encouragement are vital in every believer's life. He is the guardian of our hearts and minds, and He teaches us right from wrong.

John characterizes those who do not have an anointing of the Holy Spirit (2:20) as false prophets (4:1). They pretend to be believers (2:19), yet they propagate a false gospel (2:21). They deny Jesus as God in flesh (our only salvation!), and they reject the relationship between God the Father and God the Son (2:22). Do you see how dangerous such people can be to a pure faith? They might sound convincing, but their doctrine is full of deception.

The airwaves are filled with false teachers and manipulators of God's Word. They speak in half-truths, often quoting the Bible out of context, and they lead people toward destruction. Much of what we hear in American cultural Christianity only makes sense in our culture. It sells here, but it would never sell (or preach) in a mud hut in Africa. The gospel is for every tongue and tribe. The Spirit's work knows no economic or social boundaries, and we need Him to give us discernment.

Only through God's Word and the Holy Spirit can we determine what is true and thereby peacefully abide in the Lord. This is my appeal to you: acknowledge and appropriate the Holy Spirit. You can't live the Christian life through your own strength. By surrendering to the control of the Holy Spirit, you'll experience fullness and freedom!

THE SOON COMING OF THE SAVIOR

We know that Christ is going to return some day. What will your story be when you stand before Him? Will He condemn you for being sloppy and indifferent in your faith, or will you be praised for your passion, forgiving spirit, faithfulness and commitment to excellence in service? We're only one heartbeat away from eternity, and our experience in the afterlife is determined by how we allow Christ to live in and through us in the present. First John 2 wraps up with a command, "Now, little children, abide in Him, so that when He appears, we may have confidence and not shrink away from Him in shame at His coming" (2:28).

The word "confidence" in verse 28 could also be translated "assurance." By living in Christ, we are assured a place in His kingdom. By coming before God with nothing to hide, we can enjoy the fullness of His salvation.

John knew that the Enemy is powerful and cunning, but he also knew that we are more than conquerors through Jesus Christ. (The verb "to overcome" is found twenty-eight times in the New Testament, and twenty-four of these mentions are in John's writings.) John encouraged us to stay in the battle—relying on the Spirit and walking in the truth—so that when the Lord returns, we will be purely joyful rather than ashamed.

It's important to grasp the power we have in Christ. The game of life can be challenging, but we never have to throw everything to chance and squeak by with a last-minute 60-yard Hail Mary pass. Jesus already won the game for us. He overcame *every* fear and anxiety, and He conquered death, hell and the grave. Don't live or act like one who is going to barely get ahead in the end. "Greater is He who is in you than he who is in the world" (4:4). The end of the war has been settled in eternity past. We need to live like we're on the winning side.

Only through submitting to Christ's lordship can we abide in perfect peace. Jesus is the only One who can fill the deepest longings of a person's heart. You may be able to maintain a façade of happiness for a while, but deep inside you'll feel lonely and alone. Only through Christ's power do we find guidance and strength to walk in His will and stand on His promises.

ABIDING IN CHRIST GIVES US PURPOSE

Why are you here? What purpose do you serve? Who or what do you live for? How will you be remembered?

The two greatest days in our lives are the day we're born and the day we find out why we're alive. Believers have assurance of their purpose—to know Christ and to make Him known.

If you want to live a full, abundant life, your number one priority must be to seeking to know God and do His will. A. W. Tozer writes, "God made us for Himself; that is the first and last thing that can be said about human existence and whatever more we add is but commentary."

It's time to apply your upgrade; there's no reason to waste another day. But remember, an upgrade is not a once-and-done thing. Upgrades in Christ are continual. There's always more of His fullness to be experienced—and you grow when He abides in you and you abide in Him.

You can't be fulfilled until you're filled. In Colossians 1:9, Paul's prayer was that "you may be filled." This is an experiential filling, and several components are involved.

To be fulfilled, you need to be filled with the knowledge of God's will. The Greek word *epignosis* means "full knowledge"; it's the comprehension of God's revelation of Himself. There's a difference between knowing things intellectually and fully knowing them. When you seek to understand and follow God's will, His desires replace your own. Live up to what you know!

To be fulfilled, you need to be filled with wisdom and understanding. Spend daily time in the Word. While the Bible remains the bestselling book of all time, it's sadly one of the least read. You might own multiple translations, but they're nothing to you if you don't apply them. You need to fully develop the knowledge you have while seeking to gain more.

Some cultural Christians have just enough knowledge to make them dangerous, quoting verses out of context and building their own version of what they think faith looks like. Instead, your heart should be able to accurately comprehend the Scriptures. Do you feel as if you could never be wise? James 1:5, 6 tells us, "But if any of you lacks wisdom, let him ask of God, who gives to all generously and without reproach, and it will be given to him. But he must ask in faith without any doubting, for the one who doubts is like the surf of the sea, driven and tossed by the wind."

To be fulfilled, you need to be filled with the Spirit. I already mentioned the importance of the Spirit earlier, but His role is worth stressing again. Man can be wise in his own eyes but not in God's. Just read the book of Proverbs and you'll see hundreds of examples of this. (Several years ago I challenged our congregation to read through Proverbs every month. I still get e-mails and notes from members telling me the difference that made in their lives. They give testimonies of how it has impacted their relationships, job choices, family decisions and parenting.) You need to seriously search the Scriptures, seeking the guidance of the Holy Spirit, to comprehend God's commands and wisdom.

To be fulfilled, you need to be filled with a desire to live out what you believe. We all know that a person can be highly educated and not be able to function in the real world. Similarly, faith without works is dead (James 2:17). You can't follow God's will and stay in your own personal bubble. God will push you out of your comfort zone to go deeper, to learn more and to reach out to others in love.

Warren Wiersbe explains, "Two words summarize the practicality of the Christian life: walk and work. The sequence is important: first wisdom; then walk; then work. I cannot work for God unless I am walking with Him; but I cannot walk with Him if I am ignorant of His will."[28] When you have wisdom and understanding, you'll know how to apply what God is teaching you in your daily life.

WHAT PATH ARE YOU ON?

When Colossians 1:10 calls us to "walk in a manner worthy of the Lord," it's saying that we need to stay on the straight and narrow. Walking has the connotation of direction. We aren't supposed to meander; we're meant to daily follow God's path. Psalm 1:1–2 says, "Blessed is the man who does not walk in the counsel of the wicked, nor stand in the path of sinners, nor sit in the seat of scoffers! But his delight is in the law of the Lord, and in His law he meditates day and night."

The problem with American Christianity is that many so-called believers try to figure out how much they can act like the devil and still get into heaven. Some call this "freedom in Christ," but it's far from "in Christ." Even in churches, people brag about their "freedoms"—trying to outdo each other by being "in the world," but failing to remember that Romans 12:2 commands us, "Do not be conformed to this world, but be transformed."

We may know the grace of God, but we need to also know His will. When we pray with surrendered hearts, God fills our lives. When we submit ourselves to Him through prayer, He expresses His sovereignty over our lives and gives us an effective witness. When Paul said, "We have not ceased to pray for you" (Col. 1:9), he expressed the importance of continuous prayer.

In order to grow in the Lord, we must humble ourselves, and our prayer has to be consistent, constant and specific. There's no excuse for weak, general prayers. You have specific struggles, so pray specific prayers and trust God to give specific responses.

Christianity is most powerful when it's practical. Jesus walked and lived among the people, and they loved Him; whereas the Pharisees had big heads and cold hearts.

Reading and knowing the Word is meant to lead to an active witness. The Scriptures contain clear, practical applications for the saints. When Christ is our path, our thoughts and purposes will be pure and clear, and we will reflect who He is to a world desperately in need of a consistent witness.

YOUR PLEASURE IS IN CHRIST

Colossians tells us our desire should be for our walk to "please Him in all respects" (1:10). You can do nothing better with your life than to use it to bring glory and pleasure to the Lord.

At the beginning of each day, pray that what you do and how you do it would be pleasing to God. At the end of the day, ask the Lord if what you did and how you did it was pleasing to Him. This will help keep your sin list short!

What characterizes a life that's pleasing to God?

Your life should bear fruit. Because we have a new nature in Christ, we should exhibit His goodness. Our "fruit" is the outward expression of our inward redemption. Colossians 1:10 challenges us to live lives worthy of our calling, "bearing fruit in every good work."

Scripture often uses the fruit metaphor: "Bear fruit in keeping with repentance" (Matt. 3:8); "A good tree cannot produce bad fruit, nor can a bad tree produce good fruit" (7:18); "Each tree is known by its own fruit" (Luke 6:44); "The seed which fell among the thorns, these are the ones who have heard, and as they go on their way they are choked with worries and riches and pleasures of this life, and bring no fruit to maturity" (8:14); "Every branch in Me [Christ] that does not bear fruit, He [the Father] takes away; and every branch that bears fruit, He prunes it so that it may bear more fruit" (John 15:2); "I [Christ] am the vine, you are the branches; he who abides in Me and I in him, he bears much fruit, for apart from Me you can do nothing" (15:5).

You should walk in God's light. First John 1:7 teaches, "If we walk in the Light as He Himself is in the Light, we have fellowship with one another, and the blood of Jesus His Son cleanses us from all sin." God will always give you enough light to see the next step. Walking in the light of the Lord's wisdom begins with trusting Him with the small things. To love God is to follow Him, to follow Him is to know Him, and to know Him is to love Him. Do you see how these build on one another?

You should stand in God's strength. When we walk with the Lord, we will be "strengthened with all power, according to His glorious might" (Col. 1:11). The word "all" lets us know that we will experience the fullness of God's power, and the expression of that power is God's "glorious might." As Christ's followers, we have the power of God in us.

JUST DO IT!

When you seek God's wisdom and the fullness of His power in your life, you'll experience a spiritual upgrade like nothing you could imagine. Colossians 1:11–12 says you work "for the attaining of all steadfastness and patience" and that the end result is "joyously giving thanks to the Father, who has qualified us to share in the inheritance of the saints in Light."

The end result is fulfillment and joy though the trials and pressures of daily life. Christ gives you the powers of endurance and patience so that you can "count it all joy" when troubles come your way (James 1:2). You've been told to walk worthy. If you're not living at that level, then you're living beneath it and are missing all the privileges that come with life in Christ.

Charles Spurgeon once wrote, "Christians should have . . . such abundant life that in poverty they are rich, in sickness they are in spiritual health, in contempt they are full of triumph, and in death full of glory."[29] You can't imitate being full of the Spirit. Are you abiding in Christ and experiencing that fullness? Are you enjoying your upgrade?

A NEW PERSPECTIVE

I'VE mentioned the victorious Christian life several times throughout this book, and the "upgraded life" is exactly that—full of Christ's victory! As a pastor, I've seen people overcome addictions, affairs and attitudes that were handicapping their lives. I've also been blessed to observe countless numbers of people learn how to move from trying harder to abiding in Christ.

When I came to Sherwood as pastor, the church was very legalistic. Everywhere I turned there were rules. Realizing that legalism is bondage, I took a year and preached through Galatians. Peeling back the layers of that legalistic onion was a painful process that made me (and others) cry, but it had to be done.

People feel "safe" with rules, but rules do not lead to an upgraded life. They do just the opposite; they hold you back from all God has for you in the life of faith. The choices we make in our lives reveal where we put our faith. God challenges us to follow Him, and while this journey can be trying, it leads to joy when it's done right. The Christian life is based on the assumption that we can take God at His Word. God will not lead us off a cliff or throw us under a bus. His promises are true, and we know they can be trusted.

THE RELEVANCE

Paul wrote the letters of Ephesians, Philippians and Colossians not because the church wasn't functioning but because he wanted to encourage believers to live up to their fullness in Christ. Paul reminded us that the Christian life is not centered on feelings; it is centered on faith. Paul gave the church of the first century—and today—clear guidelines for living at the highest level. He wrote to encourage the saints to act like saints. Read Colossians 1:1–8:

> To the saints and faithful brethren in Christ who are at Colossae: Grace to you and peace from God our Father. We give thanks to God, the Father of our Lord Jesus Christ, praying always for you, since we heard of your faith in Christ Jesus and the love which you have for all the saints; because of the hope laid up for you in heaven, of which you previously heard in the word of truth, the gospel which has come to you, just as in all the world also it is constantly bearing fruit and increasing, even as it has been doing in you also since the day you heard of it and understood the grace of God in truth; just as you learned it from Epaphras, our beloved fellow bond servant, who is a faithful servant of Christ on our behalf, and he also informed us of your love in the Spirit.

Spiritually speaking, the Colossians were saints in Christ. They knew Him as their source, strength, security and sustainer. In fact we're all saints because we've been set apart—not to be weird or strange but to be transformed into the image of Christ.

Practically speaking, the Colossians were faithful, and this is an essential component of a Christ-centered life. One of the reasons believers never live at the highest level is a lack of faith-fulness. People are inconsistent in their church attendance, pray-ing, giving and serving, and then they wonder why their walk with God seems to be hit-or-miss. Love for the Lord produces loyalty, first to Christ and then to the family of faith. Continu-ous victory is contingent upon faithfulness.

The Colossians were also saints and brethren in God's fam-ily. They had a spiritual and physical address, living "in Christ" and in Colossae. We are often confused by the word "saint"; it makes us think of a "saintly" grandparent or of someone who has been sainted by the Catholic church. But that's not what the word means. "Saint" comes from the same Latin root as "to sanctify." When we're saved by Christ and filled with the Spirit, we're saints—people who receive the action of sanctification. Christ is our source and sustainer who does in us what we can't do for ourselves. If we insist on "doing faith" our way by trying harder, we aren't cooperating with Christ; we are in conflict with Him. We can never be worthy on our own; our worthiness is in who Christ is and what He has done.

THE OFFER

Just like the Colossians' culture, our world is full of false gospels. We're told that we're our own gods and that we can pick and choose our faith—and then be "blessed" materially by it. But this type of warped faith is a poor substitute for victory.

Our American culture is in awe of methods and technology. Our "stuff" can become a god. We can buy the lie that God needs aids, props and images to communicate His message. While there's nothing wrong with using those things, I have two concerns. One, it may indicate we don't think the Word and the Holy Spirit are sufficient. Two, we become more impressed with our aids and props than the power of the gospel.

At a conference a few years ago, some pastors were sitting around a table talking about ministry. Several were sharing about their churches' impressive lighting, sound and multimedia capabilities. Finally one of the pastors said, "Guys, you're all bragging about your shovels, and the point is that we're digging for gold. You're missing the gold!"

There's nothing wrong with a church keeping up with current technology. In fact, I believe God calls us to do everything with excellence. But these churches had substituted impressive shows of technology for teaching the truth, bright lights for the Light of the world, and gimmicks for godliness. Smoke and mirrors are the tools of a magician and a carnival. What we need is a power that doesn't require props.

Victory is stripped away when you stray from the truth. Paul was rightly disgusted by deviations from the gospel. In Galatians, he wrote,

> I am amazed that you are so quickly deserting Him who called you by the grace of Christ, for a different gospel; which is really not another; only there are some who are disturbing you and want to distort the gospel of Christ. But even if we, or an angel from heaven, should preach to you a gospel contrary to what we have preached to you, he is to be accursed! As we have said before, so I say again now, if any man is preaching to you a gospel contrary to what you received, he is to be accursed! (1:6–9)

Remember, the false prophets of the Old Testament told the kings and the people what they wanted to hear…and it led to defeat and captivity. What we need is truth, and sometimes truth hurts. Those who spread false gospels will flatter your ego in order to deceive you. They do it for donations, TV ratings, book sales and self-exaltation. The road of telling you what you want to hear is wide, and it will lead to defeat. You may think you're flying first-class, but one day you'll wake up to discover you're grounded. Without exception, Christ is the only true way.

The Bible is a Jesus book. You can find Jesus throughout the Scriptures. There is a scarlet thread that runs through every page. The Old Testament contains a record of the preparation for Christ's coming; the Gospels present Christ's life and miracles; Acts proclaims Christ's grace and power; the Epistles teach the personification of "Christ in you, the hope of glory" (Col. 1:27); and Revelation reveals that Christ the Lamb will overcome for all eternity.

Students of God's Word will live at a high level because they have embraced Christ's abundant, victorious life available through the Scriptures. Will you take advantage of this offer?

THE KEY

Unlike many in other parts of the world, American Christians have resources, study Bibles, church options, conferences and materials. Yet the average man never darkens the door of a Christian bookstore.

We have an incredible number of tools for growth at our disposal, but we seem to be unable or unwilling to apply them. Studies show there is little difference between the choices, lifestyles and habits of non-believers and believers. The divorce rate is nearly the same between the two groups. The percentage of church members in counseling is incredibly high. As a pastor and one who travels the country speaking in all kinds of churches, I believe I know the problem: we don't appropriate what has been given to us.

When I travel, I normally use the same airline. I want to build up my frequent-flier miles and get priority seating if possible. When it's time to board, the person at the gate says, "We will be boarding by zones, beginning with first class." Then she goes down the zones, starting with zone one, then zone two and so on. Because of my miles, I'm usually upgraded to first class or, at worse, I'm in zone one. That way I can get on the plane, find my seat and put my bags in the overhead bin before the mass of passengers hits the ramp.

Let me baptize that illustration. Because we have the indwelling Holy Spirit, we have been given the privilege of flying first class. But even with that understanding, what if you refuse to appropriate the rights and privileges earned for you by Christ? You end up being the last one to board, seated at the back of the plane, by the restroom and between a passenger with motion sickness and a woman with a screaming baby.

Paul's prayer for the Colossian believers reveals what he wanted to see happen in their lives. In verse 4, he stressed having an active faith in Christ. (This faith is no secret. In 1:5, Paul indicated that the Colossians had "previously heard the word of truth.") In verse 8, he stressed a full love for fellow saints. And in verse 5, he explained that their hope was stored up in heaven.

Paul longed for the Colossians to know God's will. Living life as God intends means a willingness to do what God says. God's Word has been given for our obedience. It is not open for debate. The Scriptures bring a sense of purpose to our lives. Paul's final plea was that the Colossians would walk in God's ways. God's way is a straight and narrow path. It has curbs to keep us from running off the road into a ditch. When God says not to do something, He is warning you of a danger ahead. When God says do something, He is giving you the freedom to get in the fast lane and move forward. He's talking about a way of life.

So how do we upgrade?

- By hearing and paying attention to the Word.
- By understanding (which involves learning from the Scriptures and praying for our knowledge to be

transformed into wisdom through the guidance and intercession of the Spirit).

- By continuously growing and never settling where we are in our faith. God always has more in store.
- By believing that what God has said is true.
- By doing. We need to act on the commands God has given us!

THE CHOICE

You make choices every day. You choose to exercise or not. You choose where to go when you eat out. You choose the amount of time you spend on the Internet. You choose where you live, what you do and how you do it. And the choice is yours today—will you start living up to your potential in Christ, or will you continue trying to figure out life and faith in your own strength?

Victory has been offered to you. Through Christ, you have the key to your upgrade. But you still have to make a decision—will you walk in victory or settle for defeat?

It's common to see sports teams start doing poorly in their season and give up. They accept loss as their norm and stop striving to do their best. As I'm wrapping up this chapter, the New York Giants have just defeated the New England Patriots in Super Bowl XLVI. It's the first time in Super Bowl history that a 9-7 team went all the way and won the NFL Championship. It was an unlikely story. After a four-game losing streak and losing five games in six weeks, the Giants had been written off by most sports writers and fans. There was talk of letting their head coach go. Their quarterback Eli Manning was criticized for saying he belonged in the category of elite quarterbacks. Then something clicked. According to ESPN, a school teacher came in to lead chapel and talked to the team about being "all in," using the poker term as an illustration. He said there comes a time when you have to believe enough in what you are doing to go "all in." The talk worked. Despite the season's injuries, lackluster running game and outside critiques, the team came together and dominated their opponents, winning five road games in a row.

While I'm not endorsing gambling or poker, the concept of "all in" is a valid one when thinking about living a victorious life. There comes a time when you have to stop playing around the edges and get in the game. To walk in victory, you have to get out of the pew and onto the field. You've got to engage and lay everything on the line. Unfortunately, most will settle for being spectators in the great game of life. They will choose to run hot and cold, take three steps forward and five backward and never make real progress because they've never been "all in" with Jesus.

Christ has called His saints to victory. Stay on track, and the power of the Holy Spirit will enable you to overcome difficulties and walk according to the Word. How visible is Christ's power in your life? You likely fall into one of three categories.

Christ might be present in your life. You've received Christ, but you don't have His power because—for some reason such as sin, apathy or a stronghold that is controlling you—He's being restricted from truly working in your life. Will you make the choice to turn *everything* over to Him and to identify yourself as one of His followers?

Christ might be prominent in your life. You aren't afraid for people to know that you're a believer, but you haven't completely accepted Him as Lord. Will you surrender your will and self-centered desires and humble yourself to take on anything Christ asks of you?

Christ might be preeminent in your life. You have tested God and found Him to be faithful and true. You trust the Lord as your source of life and find complete sufficiency in Him.

I pray that you fall into the final category. If you don't, what's holding you back? Christ has done His part. Now you have to make the choice to accept His victory and all the responsibilities and blessings that come along with it.

THE VICTORIOUS UPGRADE

There's a popular hymn called "Victory in Jesus." Sadly, more people are probably familiar with the lyrics than with Christ's victory. But the truth remains—there is true victory in Christ. It isn't an occasional win followed by several crippling defeats. It's victory on a daily basis.

I pray you have been challenged to seek more of God so He can upgrade your life to make you more like Himself. The key isn't trying—it's trusting. Christ has already defeated everything that's defeating you. Will you choose to upgrade to His freeing victory?

A. W. Tozer wrote,

> Most of the great religions of the world begin with externals…the starting point is usually with diet, dress, ascetic practices or the celebration of days. Then the hope is that somehow by the performance of external acts they will be able to work in on themselves to the heart…That is exactly contrary to the Scriptures. To begin on the outside and then work into the center is unknown to the New Testament. This was the difference between our Lord Jesus Christ and the Pharisees. The Pharisees were concerned about the exterior, while Jesus majored on the internal. The Pharisees thought that by practicing external things they could change their internal. Jesus knew better and challenged this position throughout His ministry. He taught that it was the heart that mattered. The internal matters, and when the internal is right, the outside will fall into line perfectly.[30]

Your upgraded life begins on the inside. God is calling you to respond. What's it going to be?

Endnotes

Chapter 1

1. William Temple, *The Hope of a New World* (New York: The Macmillan Company, 1942), 30.

Chapter 2

2. *Easton's 1897 Bible Dictionary*. Thomas Nelson, s.v. "repentance," accessed September 01, 2022 via dictionary.com, http://dictionary.reference.com/browse/repentance.

3. Sometimes you're going to be the Nathan, so remember that rebuke needs to be done in love. People wrapped up in sin are usually guarded and not easily approachable. They tend to use lines like, "Look, it's my life. It's none of your business," or "I've prayed about this and have peace about it, so back off." This is a load of garbage, but you can't force others to repent. Instead you need to remain a constant presence, continually praying for them. In the meantime, you need to keep your heart right before the Lord. He may need to deal with something in you before He can use you to minister to another.

4. Elizabeth R. Skoglund, *Wounded Heroes* (Grand Rapids: Ravens Ridge Books, 1992).

Chapter 3

5. E.M. Bounds, *The Necessity of Prayer* (New Kensington, PA: Whitaker House, 1987).

6. Vance Havner, *Repent or Else!* (Grand Rapids: Revell, 1958).

7. Chris Wright, *Experiencing God: Psalm 119* (Leicester: Religious and Theological Studies Fellowship, 2000).

Chapter 4

8. John Wesley, "The Circumcision of the Heart," preached at St. Mary's in Oxford on January 1, 1733, http://new.gbgm-umc.org/umhistory/wesley/sermons/17/.

9.   John Phillips, *Exploring Ephesians and Philippians: An Expository Commentary* (Grand Rapids: Kregel Publications, 1995), p. 130.

10.   Frederick Buchner, *Beyond Words* (San Francisco: Harper, 2004), 18.

Chapter 5

11.   Philip Elmer-DeWitt, "Piper Jaffray: iPad 2 totally sold out, 70% to new buyers," *Fortune* (March 13, 2011): accessed December 17, 2011, http://tech.fortune.cnn.com/2011/03/13/piper-jaffray-ipad-2-totally-sold-out-70-to-new-buyers/.

12.   Phillip Keller, *Joshua: Mighty Warrior and Man of Faith* (Grand Rapids: Kregel Publications, 1983).

13.   John Bisagno, *Life Without Compromise* (Nashville: Broadman Press, 1982).

14.   J. Oswald Sanders, *Spiritual Leadership: Principles of Excellence for Every Believer* (Chicago: Moody, 2007).

15.   Francis Schaeffer, *Joshua and the Flow of Biblical History* (Wheaton, IL: Crossway Books, 2004).

16.   Alan Redpath, *Victorious Christian Living: Studies in the Book of Joshua* (Grand Rapids: Revell, 1993).

Chapter 7

17.   A.T. Pierson, *The Acts of the Holy Spirit* (Grand Rapids: Revell, 1895), 19.

18.   Warren Wiersbe, *Be Real: Turning from Hypocrisy to Truth* (The BE Series Commentary) (Colorado Springs: David C. Cook, 1972).

Chapter 8

19.   A.T. Robertson, *Word Pictures in the New Testament* (Nashville: B&H Publishing, 2000).

20.   Max Lucado, *A Gentle Thunder: Hearing God Through the Storm*, (Nashville: Thomas Nelson, 1995).

21.   Warren Wiersbe, *Bible Exposition Commentary, Old Testament*, accessed via WORDsearch.

22. Phillip Keller, *A Shepherd Looks at Psalm 23* (Grand Rapids: Zondervan, 2008).

23. Ray C. Stedman, "The Shepherd and His Sheep": accessed February 12, 2012, http://www.raystedman.org/new-testament/john/the-shepherd-and-his-sheep.

24. Max Lucado, "For Longer than Forever: The God Who Loves Boldly" in *A Gentle Thunder* (Nashville: Thomas Nelson, 2009).

Chapter 9

25. Many of my thoughts on this passage have been gleaned from reading authors' thoughts from another era. Most of the books written today seem to avoid the simple words of those great writers. But I feel that short, concise and powerful truths are just what we simple sheep need to hear and incorporate into our lives. (Several great pastors' teachings can be found on 2ProphetU.com. I encourage you to check out the valuable resources on this website!)

26. William Butler Yeats, *Autobiographies* (New York: Scribner, 1999), 385.

Chapter 10

27. The devil wants us to try to get by on our own fleshly strength, wisdom and abilities, but we can't do anything without God's help. The devil can never be trusted! We hear Satan's voice three times in the Scriptures. In Genesis he slandered God to man. In Job he slandered man to God. And in Matthew he came against Jesus, the Son of God and the Son of Man. In Matthew we learn that we should be aware of the devil's devices. We should be prepared so that we can see his attacks coming and avoid them and their devastating effects.

28. Warren Wiersbe, *The Bible Exposition Commentary*, vol. 2, The New Testament (Colorado Springs: David C. Cook, 2001), 111.

29. Charles Spurgeon, "Life More Abundant: A Sermon Delivered on Lord's-Day Morning, January 4, 1874": accessed January 11, 2012, http://www.spurgeongems.org/vols19-21/chs1150.pdf.

Chapter 11

30. A. W. Tozer, *Living as a Christian*, ed. James L. Snyder (Ventura, CA: Regal, 2009) 64–65.

"For Those Who Thirst for Revival"

Pastors from all over the country are refreshed at these annual conferences (in Albany, GA and Pigeon Forge, TN) focused on revival and the victorious Christian life. Interested in attending?

Check out **http://www.refreshconference.org/** for dates and details!

Want to read more about upgrading from adequacy to abundance in the Spirit?

Visit **www.michaelcatt.com** for thoughts from the cluttered desk of Michael Catt.

This book was produced by CLC Publications. We hope it has been life-changing and has given you a fresh experience of God through the work of the Holy Spirit. CLC Publications is an outreach of CLC Ministries International, a global literature mission with work in over fifty countries. If you would like to know more about us or are interested in opportunities to serve with a faith mission, we invite you to contact us at:

CLC Ministries International
PO Box 1449
Fort Washington, PA 19034

Phone: 215-542-1242
E-mail: orders@clcpublications.com
Website: www.clcpublications.com

DO YOU LOVE GOOD CHRISTIAN BOOKS?
Do you have a heart for worldwide missions?

You can receive a FREE subscription to
CLC's newsletter on global literature missions
Order by e-mail at:

clcworld@clcusa.org
Or fill in the coupon below and mail to:

**PO Box 1449
Fort Washington, PA 19034**

FREE *CLC WORLD* SUBSCRIPTION!

Name: _____

Address:_____

_____

Phone: _____ E-mail:_____

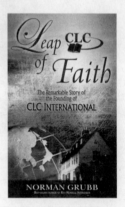

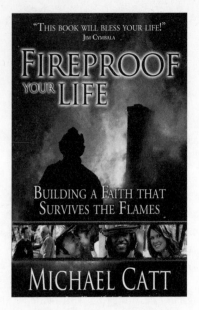

FIREPROOF YOUR LIFE

Michael Catt

Using illustrations from his own life and from the movie *Fireproof*, Catt discusses practical issues such as temptation, marriage and finances, helping us build a faith that resists our corrosive culture. Rather than succumb to the pressure of circumstances, we can stand tall and face our challenges in Christ's power.

Life's trials can *overcome* us—or they can *serve* us, growing us into the mature, life-giving believers God intends.

ISBN: 978-0-87508-984-3